CW01081810

LIKE A SHADOW

ALSO BY TAMARACK SONG

A Forest Bathing Companion
Learn About Nature's Rejuvenating Powers On a Healing Nature Trail Walk

The Healing Nature Trail
Forest Bathing for Recovery and Awakening

Truthspeaking
Ancestral Ways to Hear and Speak the Voice of the Heart

Blossoming the Child
A Guide to Primal Parenting

Fat Moons and Hunger Moons
The Turn of the Seasons for Northwoods Natives

Becoming Nature
Learning the Language of Wild Animals and Plants

Entering the Mind of the Tracker
*Native Practices for Developing Intuitive
Consciousness and Discovering Hidden Nature*

Essential Zen
3000 Morsels That Have Guided–and Perplexed–Seekers throughout the Ages

Zen Rising
366 Sage Stories to Enkindle Your Days

Song of Trusting the Heart
A Classic Zen Poem for Daily Meditation

Whispers of the Ancients
Native Tales for Teaching and Healing in Our Time

Journey to the Ancestral Self
The Native Lifeway Guide for Living in Harmony with the Earth Mother

Extreme Survival Meat
A Guide for Safe Scavenging, Pemmican Making, and Roadkill

Wilderness Stress and Trauma
Management Protocols for Instructors, Guides, and Adventurers

The Wilderness Stress and Trauma Workbook
A Quick-Reference and Training Guide

Becoming You
3 Steps to Emotional Freedom and What Keeps You from It

See www.snowwolfpublishing.org for an updated list of Tamarack's publications.

LIKE A SHADOW

THE LIFE AND TRAINING OF A GUARDIAN WARRIOR

TAMARACK SONG

Snow Wolf Publishing

SNOW WOLF PUBLISHING
7124 Military Road
Three Lakes, Wisconsin 54562
www.snowwolfpublishing.org

Snow Wolf Publishing is a division of Teaching Drum Outdoor School

Copyright © 2020 by Tamarack Song

All rights reserved. No part of this book may be reproduced or utilized in any form or by any means, electronic or mechanical, including photocopying, recording, or by any information storage and retrieval system, without first obtaining written permission from the publisher.

Song, Tamarack, 1948 –
Like a Shadow: The Life and Training of a Guardian Warrior

ISBN: 978-0-9966561-1-5

Text design and layout by JaadBookDesign.com

To send correspondence to the author of this book, mail a first class letter to the author c/o Snow Wolf Publishing, 7124 Military Road, Three Lakes, Wisconsin 54562, and we will forward the communication; or email the author at info@snowwolfpublishing.org.

Visit the author's websites at www.healingnaturecenter.org, www.teachingdrum.org, and www.snowwolfpublishing.org.

References to Internet websites (URLs) were accurate at the time of writing. Neither the authors nor Snow Wolf Publishing are responsible for URLs that may have expired or changed since this book was published.

CONTENTS

GUARDIAN ETHICS

Ever at the forefront of Guardian Consciousness is the ultimate Mission of the Guardian: to serve his/her community. The tactics of stealth, deception, and disabling presented in this book are intended to be used only on Missions, and only for the Greater Good. Neither the author nor anyone associated with him condone the use of Guardian implements or methodologies in ways that would cause others harm.

DEDICATION

Thomas (left) with Tamarack at their training camp.

Thomas Seibold embodied the Guardian archetype in every-thing he did. He was an exemplary Trainee, and later he became a valued member of my staff. I cherish my memories of the two of us absorbed in craftwork while we talked late into the night about the renewal of vital Native Lifeway skills and awarenesses.

I last saw Thomas in the late spring of 2012, when he left for a solo adventure in Alaska's Brooks Range Wilderness. He never came back, and the extensive searches we fielded did not yield enough clues to tell us why.

If Thomas were still with us, I have no doubt that he would be an intrinsic part of the resurgence of the Guardian Way that this book reflects. With deep regard for my clan brother, I dedicate this book not only to his memory, but to his living spirit. He continues to be an inspiration for those of us who recount the stories of his adventures. As his presence emanates from the pages of this book, I trust that he will also evoke the spirit of the Guardian in you.

PART I

THE CALLING

The Maori word for *Guardian** is *kaitiakitanga*. 'Kai' means *food for soul, body, and mind*; 'tiaki' refers to *caretaking*; and 'tanga' is *the people*.[1] For *Natives*,** everything is an expression of life and all life is related. *The people*, then, refers to the plant people, the rock people, and the animal people — which includes insects, fish, reptiles, birds, and humans.

Kaitiakitanga perfectly describes the role of the Guardian: answering the call to help maintain *Balance* between the people and the land. In doing so, the Guardian tends to the welfare of all creatures who live here on Earth.

---

* Glossary terms are italicized the first time they appear.
** Native here indicates a person living a hunter-gatherer lifestyle.

CHAPTER 1

WHO IS THE GUARDIAN WARRIOR?

Some call them *Scouts*, many call them *Warriors*, and others know them as *Protectors*. To Native people, they are *Guardians*: the manifestation of the band's courage, selflessness, and desire to serve. Guardians can be female or male,* old or young. Invisible, alert, and unbiased, they serve as sentries, wayfinders, messengers, ambassadors, sleuths, defenders, providers, and mentors. Their presence gives peace of mind to their people, so that they can comfortably pursue their day's activities and rest peacefully in the night.

In this day, Guardians are again needed by their people and their Mother Earth—perhaps more than ever. This book guides you to where they can be found. You may be surprised to discover just how close one lives to your heart, and how big a part she already plays in your life.

When I am asked whether or not I am a Guardian, I often hesitate, as I have yet to come up with a short and easy answer. This is one of the reasons I have embarked on the journey of creating this book. As you'll see, the response I have come up with is neither short nor easy.

When many of us think of the Guardian, we picture a mythical figure created out of our incomplete and filtered perceptions of *Native Lifeway*. We see them as bold, stoic, and masters of

---

* I will alternate my use of "he" and "she" pronouns to describe Guardians.

the art of combat. If I held that image, I would have to answer "No" to the question of whether or not I am a Guardian. However, if I had time to reflect on who the Guardian actually is and explain it, my answer would be a resounding "Yes!"

The Truth Behind the Image

Webster's Third New International Dictionary defines a *Warrior* as "a man engaged or experienced in warfare and especially in primitive warfare or the close combat of ancient or medieval times," and "a person of demonstrated courage, fortitude, zeal, or pugnacity."[2] This is a stereotypical image of the Warrior, perpetuated by:

- The imbalanced life of a Native Warrior when flung into the onslaught of Civilization
- *Civilized** people's tendency to romanticize their colonization of Native Peoples
- The liberal view of the Warrior as the embodiment of Native resistance to Civilization

Yet Webster's Dictionary's portrayal of the Warrior makes sense when we look at the situation: His people, his lifeway, and his Mother Earth are under siege, so he is naturally in a state of constant preparedness for war.

Here we run head-on into a paradox, as the *Guardian Warrior* does not seek confrontation. To choose fighting as a means of resolving conflict would imperil him and compromise his ability to protect his people. As like begets like, his engagement in confrontation would inevitably draw his people into confrontation. For this reason, he engages in conflict only as a last resort.

---

* Civilized here indicates the lifestyle that results from living out of Balance; characterized by isolation from Nature, environmental degradation, regimentation, hierarchical structures, materialism, and loss of individuality.

Another Way the Image Was Created

Sadly, some of our pioneer forebears preferred genocide to diplomacy. Is it then any wonder that they would come to know the Guardian Warrior as a raging fighter?

The same Webster's dictionary defines a *Guardian* as "one that guards or secures; one to whom a person or thing is committed for protection, security, or preservation."[3] That is more in line with the traditional meaning of *Warrior* than the "man engaged or experienced in warfare" definition. The *Guardian* definition, then, is the one I will explore, and I stress the term *Guardian* rather than *Warrior* to capture the essence of this calling.

The Person

All people, including our animal, plant, and mineral kin, need protection at times, for a variety of reasons. It could be shelter from the weather or a natural disaster, from an enemy, from the burdens of family or society, or even from ourselves. The Guardian is trained to serve in all of these ways. Perhaps most importantly, she safeguards the well-being of her people by helping to assure a low level of stress and a high level of personal satisfaction. She fills in when parents need a helping hand. She defends someone who is being persecuted or falsely accused. She stands up for the exploited and the disadvantaged. She protects people from their own follies, short-sightedness, and errors of judgment. Because she functions from a place of great perspective, she can sometimes foresee peril that looms ahead.

When a Guardian meets conflict on a *Mission*, her high degree of *training* in methods of camouflage, avoidance, and deception allows her to minimize her impact upon others and their *Paths*. She has a highly attuned understanding that the life force in others is the same as the life force that flows through her, so she grants those who attempt to block her Path the utmost respect and space. If there is no other way to navigate around them, she removes them in the most efficient, least harmful way possible. When she has no choice but to fight, she does not pit herself *against* anything or anyone, but rather she battles essentially *for* Balance, relationship, and the well-being of all life.

The Way of the Guardian is the manifestation of a life lived in Balance. It represents the greatest giving: the gift of self. The Guardian and all she does centers on respect—the deepest reverence for the Earth and all She encompasses.

The Guardian is a highly attuned physical and psycho-emotional being who exemplifies the role of a benevolent yet detached shadow-like presence in Native culture. This element of the Native psyche dwells in all people, including us, to varying degrees, regardless of age or gender or how far removed we are from our Native roots.

Where We Fit

> *I see myself as a Guardian-in-training. Training is life for the Guardian, and training continues for life. I would be honored to have you join me on this sacred journey to serving all beings.*

The Calling

Those of us within Civilized cultures can easily misunderstand how a Guardian comes to be. We see our primary occupations as professions, which we choose based upon our interests, skills, and talents. We may also take income-earning potential and family traditions into account. We tend to use these same lenses when viewing the roles of Native People, which is unfortunate because it distorts the picture.

A Native Person does not have a profession, in the sense of performing one specific job day after day, year after year, for reimbursement. There are no healers, lodgebuilders, or Warriors that parallel our doctors, carpenters, and soldiers. Natives have no need for such a thing, as their means of sustenance is provided by the Earth, and their daily lives involve various activities directly necessary for the survival and well-being of their community.

If you were to ask a Native to give his profession, he might answer that it is to serve his people. In doing so, he demonstrates a variety of skills and interests, depending upon need and circumstance. A woman skilled at delivering babies would not identify herself as a midwife, as she may go for a moon or more without being called upon to assist with a birth. In the meantime, she could be tanning hides, making fish nets, drying food, or participating in any number of other activities.

The same is true of a person who serves as a Guardian. As a generalist rather than a specialist, he does not choose the special ways in which he serves his people. He doesn't even choose to function as a Guardian; he is chosen. It may be by an *Elder* who recognizes his unfolding role, or he could receive direct guidance from the Spirit World. An older Guardian might recognize another of his kind in a newborn, or someone may be given a prophetic dream of a youngster's destiny to be a Guardian.

Yet more often than not, a Native discovers his calling through personal revelation early in adolescence. He and his people view it as his destiny. He must act on it, as he does not see the option of choosing another Path. Nor does he desire anything else, as he feels deeply honored to have been chosen to serve his people in this sacred way.

The Training

If I can outrun someone, it's not necessarily because I am faster or stronger or younger. It is more likely because I can draw upon the energy of my breath, I know how to pace myself, and

I can conserve energy with effective breathing and foot placement. It may also be because I have trained myself to function well for long periods of time without food and water, and I have taught myself to sleep in the way that gives me the deep rest needed to carry on sustained activity.

The focus of Guardian Training in *Old Way* cultures is not to make you bigger, stronger, faster, or braver, but rather to make you successful. In real life, this Training is shy of the glamorous skills depicted by Hollywood movies, popular books, and mystery-enshrouded teachers. You won't learn how to defeat your enemy with one finger, see through solid objects, or swallow poison like it is no more than sugar.

The skills that truly empower do not inflate the *ego* (our fear-based identity); they bring it to rest. They do not give you dominion, but rather a sense of humility. You gain something far more valuable than grandstanding—you get the cunning and vitality to be effective. You develop the type of muscular strength that makes you quick, as well as powerful. You learn to see beyond the reach of your eyes, and to know another's thoughts and feelings as clearly as if they were your own.

Believe it or not, these are innate skills and abilities that you already possess. They have simply atrophied from lack of use. The purpose of the awarenesses and exercises in this guide is to rectify this condition by restoring your true Nature—your Guardian self.

"But What If I'm Not a Guardian?"

Even though you may not have been formally called to the Guardian Way, you—and all of us—possess the Guardian skill set, at least to some degree. Natives, you will remember, are generalists, so they train to be able to do some of everything. They can then serve their people in whatever capacity is needed. We are following suit.

The Guardian is trained to function from her center, or what the Native Elders call the *Heart-of-Hearts*. Her emotions can serve rather than control her. She disciplines herself to never act out of anger, lust, or grief, and to never lash out in rage.

If and when she finds herself in such a state of overwhelming emotion, she withdraws and re-centers herself in her Heart-of-Hearts. She knows that she is out of Balance and has temporarily lost her critical senses of perspective and attunement. She knows that she is not capable of serving, as she is wrapped up in herself and blinded to all but her own state of being. On top of that, her emotions have narrowed her vision, which makes her extremely vulnerable.

Training is never complete. The way to becoming a Guardian is continuous, without respite. One does not transform into a final Guardian state upon achieving some level of development. The process of becoming is more like an endless upriver paddle, with new springs and feeder streams to discover around every bend.

Even when there is no specific task at hand, the Guardian continually directs her energy in the most efficient, respectful, and purposeful way. She knows that the flow and process of the moment is all that there is, so she never ceases to honor it by being fully engaged.

For the Guardian, *life is training and training is life*. This is the secret to being always ready to serve. A Guardian lives on the edge: ever inquisitive, continually exploring, challenging herself, and finding ways to give thanks. In doing so, the Guardian never ceases to test her limits, strengthen her skills, expand her awareness, and attune to her environment. When there is no present challenge, she creates one, purely for the sake of being challenged.

As the Guardian becomes more empowered through training, she also becomes more gentle. The better she comes to know herself, the more selfless she grows to be. The more she dives into Chaos, the more she immerses herself in Balance.

The Awakening

This training guide details a full set of Guardian operative skills, covering all that is needed to carry out a wide variety of covert defensive, reconnaissance, supply, and recovery Missions. Yet that is not enough. To use the skills effectively, you also need the consciousness-raising and psycho-emotional honing exercises that you'll find peppered throughout the book. With all of this together, along with your dedication to the Guardian Way, you will be able to prepare yourself to serve in whatever capacity is needed by your people.

Here is an overview of what you will learn to do:

- Integrate Guardian Training with everyday life and activities.
- Function at peak level without needing to be emotion- or ally-fueled.
- Release yourself from limiting beliefs.
- Replace trust with knowing.
- Become failure-proof by eliminating chance and mistakes.
- Succeed without creating conflict or needing agreement.
- Break limiting patterns and become adaptive.
- Become aware of everything around you, so you'll no longer be surprised.
- Use problems to find solutions, and create options where there aren't any.
- Deliberately lose in order to gain more than if you won.
- Shun security to become more alert.
- Always hold the advantage.
- Stay limber and responsive—and avoid the ills of repetitive-motion training.
- Increase lung capacity and run long distances without getting winded.

- Have a rug train you to become invulnerable.
- Master at-home training with jigsaw puzzles, nut cracking, and label peeling.
- Use shame to develop a solid sense of presence.
- Make any exercise a Guardian Training.
- Set up an invisible camp.
- Execute a covert Mission by becoming invisible and disguising your actions.
- Assure Mission safety and success.
- Signal silently and effectively.
- Handle being discovered without breaking your cover.
- Help your adversaries defeat themselves with their own energy.
- Use *Mental Mastery* to unarm someone with a weapon.

The Guardian in Community

In a Native community, every person's role is valued for its essential contribution to the well-being of the group. Because of the circular nature of Native Lifeway, the role of one individual is no more or less important than the role of another. The Civilized Way, on the other hand, is structured as a pyramid, with those perceived by others to be most important at the top. Individuals and groups farther down the pyramid are largely nameless, faceless cogs in the wheel.

Ironically, the pyramid crumbles without the compliance of those at the bottom, yet those at the top typically consider them to be expendable and easily replaced.

Rather than being hierarchical, the Native Way is circular and cohesive. It recognizes the inherent worth of all members of the community. The *Circle* is only as strong as its weakest link. The independence, creativity, and initiative of each individual are encouraged, as each person's skills and perspectives are needed for the Circle to thrive.

Community members can be thought of as organs within an organism. The liver, heart, and lungs each contribute their unique gifts to the well-being of the whole. Without any one of them, the whole cannot function properly, if at all.

In the *Circle Way*, as within the human body, this interdependence fosters a state of perfect synergy. Each individual's contribution is magnified by the group, so that what the group gives back to the person is greater than what she could provide for herself. The group benefits similarly from the individual.

Some people believe that the Guardian holds a special place of honor in a Native community. It is true that she is esteemed by her people, yet so is everyone else. Each person is valued for his or her unique service to the community.

Civilized community relationships tend to be based on obedience, conformity, and a reward-sanction system to reinforce the pyramid. This encourages dependent and oppressive affiliations. Native communities urge their members to follow their personal callings and develop their unique talents to the fullest. The resulting interdependent relationships foster mutual trust and respect.

Our Training here is based on the Native model of community. The exercises are embedded in a sense of common purpose, with each exercise designed to further your personal development and unveil your unique gifts.

Imagine that the Elder Guardians have just called you to join them and the other Trainees at the secluded Guardian Training Camp they have set up some distance from the community. You are both ecstatic and humbled, as you have been waiting for this longer than you can remember. You know in the core of your being that you are in for the experience of a lifetime.

While in training, I encourage you to do as the Elders have instructed me: Always conduct yourself with integrity. Engage in each exercise as though it is your last opportunity to practice it—as though it is your entire reason for being. Carry this approach with you throughout the Training and you will come to know yourself like never before, because you will *be* like never before. Even more, you will have this profound gift—the gift of self—to bring to your people.

Part 1 / Chapter 1 Citations

1　From my personal discussion with Maria Deutsch, co-director of Growing Dialogue in New Zealand.
2　*Webster's Third New International Dictionary of the English Language, Unabridged,* s.v. "Warrior."
3　*Webster's Third,* s.v. "Guardian."

CHAPTER 2

WHY GUARDIAN TRAINING?

I'm often asked this question, but for very different reasons. Some people are genuinely curious about why I would offer such a comprehensive and in-depth program to people I hardly know. Others are skeptical, wondering if the effort and dedication demanded by the program are worth their time. They're either not convinced they will benefit personally from the teachings or they doubt the teachings will make enough of a difference in serving others.

Then there are a few people who fail to see the relevance of the topic at all. In their view, the Guardian archetype is a romantic notion from the past or an unrealistic ideal for people who crave a challenge. Still others believe the training centers on self-defense or teaches survivalists to prepare for the collapse of Civilization.

As anyone participating in Guardian Training discovers, we each have the power to create our own reality. Any of the above scenarios could fit for some people. However, the reasons we embark on a course of Guardian Training go beyond our perceived realities. The Training serves as:

- **An answer to an inner calling** that manifests itself regardless of the state of the world or any of its people

- **A pathway to becoming a complete person** by realizing our full potential for awareness, health, performance, success, and peace

■ **A way to effectively serve our people and our planet**
by equipping us with the skills to make a difference

Why Now?

The Guardian Way faded along with many other features of life
as we once knew it. Contributing factors included:

■ The rise of the hierarchical nation-state

■ The transition from nomadic adventurism to sedentary
monotony

■ The war on Nature

■ Conformity and the resulting loss of relevance for the
individual

Whether the decline of the Guardian Way allowed such a
state to occur, or instead resulted from it, is up for debate. But
one thing is certain—*the return of the Guardian Way is a powerful force for restoring Balance*, both to the human condition
and to the condition of our dear plant and animal kin. We are
on the cusp of a great resurgence of *Guardian Consciousness*,
and it is showing itself in many ways around us. You might feel
it within yourself, and you have most likely heard stories or witnessed it firsthand. Guardians are performing successful Missions for downtrodden people, for neighborhoods in crisis, for
endangered species, and for many other beings—sometimes in
defiance of all odds.

But What About Me?

Despite the focus on serving our people and our Mother Earth,
Guardian Training still begins with the question, "What's in it
for me?" In fact, it *has* to begin there. Even though the Training
is not ultimately about me, I start by focusing on myself. Some
immediate gratification aids my motivation.

Focusing on myself at the start of my Training does not mean
that I am selfish or ego-centered; on the contrary, I am closely

considering how I want to live my life. After all, who doesn't yearn to be healthy, peaceful, and self-fulfilled? Who wouldn't love to be filled with gratefulness for what he does? And what person doesn't want to be fueled with the clarity to do it?

As important as personal fulfillment is for the Guardian, there is an even more fundamental reason for putting ourselves first at the beginning: Goodness within us allows us to give it to others. When I was a young man training under Native Elders, they taught me that to be a role model for my people, I first needed to fully develop the Guardian Way within myself. They talked about the seventh generation, which is made up of those who follow in our footsteps over the years. "You're doing it for them," the Elders would say, "but first you have to do it for you."

The narratives we weave of our own lives are the example and inspiration that we will later share with others. Long after we're gone, our exploits will be retold; in this way, we live on and keep guiding. After all, everything we do is a story, as the Elders explained, and people learn best through stories.

The Direct Benefits

The Training program outlined in this book can do wonders for you as an individual. As you progress on your Guardian journey, you may notice that you feel better than you have in years. Your mind, your body, and your life purpose may all align, perhaps for the first time. Some of my Trainees describe a feeling of lightness at the beginning of their Training unlike anything they have previously experienced.

However, keep in mind that the main reward of achieving a state of Guardian Consciousness is that you are then able to share these benefits with others. Always remember that *the Guardian's role is to serve,* and everything you experience is ultimately for that purpose.

Physical Health

The true measure of a training program is whether or not the teachings continue long after the training is over. When you're young, you're nearly invincible—your body can take all kinds of abuse and bounce back fairly easily. But what about twenty, thirty, and forty years later? Don't you still want to be at your peak, feeling healthy and fully capable of serving?

With the Guardian Training approach, you could do more push-ups and chin-ups in your seventies than when you were twenty. You could have people half your age struggling to keep up with you while running. Your cardiovascular system and joints could be on a par with those of a healthy thirty-year-old. You could have half again the lung capacity of the average person your age, and you could heal from injuries considerably faster. Imagine having perfect cholesterol and blood pressure readings, with the strong and steady pulse of a marathon runner—even though you don't run marathons. You could maintain the same weight as when you were in your twenties—or be at your ideal weight if you were overweight or underweight. When necessary, you could stay active from dawn till dusk without needing caffeine or other stimulants. I and many others have seen it done with this Training.

The bottom line is that Guardian Training will not only have you feeling at your physical prime while you're a Trainee, but it will empower you to perform at your best far into the future.

Mental Health

Imagine being able to express yourself and listen so well that you could have a decades-long intimate relationship with no arguments. With a solid emotional presence, you can stay centered in the midst of Chaos. When others give in to fiery bursts of ego and temper, you exercise your well-developed capacity to be kind and empathetic.

Because you took care of yourself and trained well, you learned long ago how to take personal responsibility for your life. Instead of continuing to play the blame-shame game, you approach each potential conflict with patience and understanding. Your Training allows you to make a difference—not only for yourself, but for your people and this world.

Skill Level

I watched an older Trainee hit the bull's-eye of a target the first time he ever fired a gun, and his second shot left no trace because he placed the bullet in the same hole as the first. He played the *Secret Stone Game*, where you need to use your power of intuition to help a new player win, and he got a perfect score three times in a row. (You can find the game on page 152 of my book *Becoming Nature: Learning the Language of Wild Animals and Plants*.) He played a beanbag toss game for the first time, with five seasoned players in their prime, and he scored three-quarters of the total points.

Perceived limitations are created out of fear. The Guardian credits his Elders, his fellow Guardians, and Nature's teachings for helping him work through imagined boundaries and excel in nearly anything he attempts.

Yet Winning Isn't Everything

A more typical practice of the Guardian than playing to win is *playing to lose*, but just barely. The real skill lies in keeping the game close enough to be competitive, yet not too close that you could end up winning. In the example I just gave of the guy who buried one bullet atop the other, he could have chosen a spot on the outer edge of the target for his second shot. Then he could have passed off his first shot as beginner's luck, which would have kept the target shooting competitive.

In spite of how it might appear, the Guardian's intent is not to deceive or harm his opponent, but rather to deceive *himself*, to keep *himself* on his toes. He is showing himself what he is capable of even more so than by winning, as it takes a more highly developed skill set to barely keep from winning than to win outright.

And he is helping to train other Guardians. Fully developing his own talents and ability to perform is crucial to bringing out the best in someone else. "Deceiving" the opponent by making it appear he wants to win creates a competitive environment for the opponent to strengthen her skills—and feel good about herself in the process. He is serving his fellow Trainee through this four-step process:

1. **Putting his ego aside**
2. **Gaining self-satisfaction** in knowing his abilities without needing to prove them
3. **Creating space** for others to develop their potentials
4. **Helping others gain the confidence** and perspective to serve

When the intention is not to win and the ego is not allowed to take over, one can then effortlessly win the game when winning is desired. Yet win or lose, the true benefit for the Guardian lies in helping others.

The same play-to-lose approach can be applied to team performance. The senior Guardian works covertly to help the other team win, without letting even her own team members catch on to her intent. To do that, everyone must believe that she is giving her all to win—which in essence she is. In doing so, she embodies two seemingly conflicting personas simultaneously: the ruse of the determined competitor externally and the detached Zen Master internally.

With what I call *Ruse Training*, the Guardian's *shadow skills* come into play. It takes great deceptive ability to create a façade believable enough to allow the serving of the *Greater Good* (the best possible outcome for the greatest number of people, regardless of relationship) without being detected. Whether those façades are *smokescreens*, diversions, or false identities, Ruse Training is excellent preparation.

Playing to lose exemplifies the spirit of the Guardian Way. Perhaps more than any other, this Guardian skill shows that we are here on Earth not for personal gain. If we were, we would go ahead and win to savor the glory and reward. Nor are we here to promote any personal belief. If we were, we would use our abilities to further our philosophy. Rather, we play to lose in order to:

- **Hone** our ability to serve whomever, wherever, and whenever needed
- **Help** others reach their full potentials
- **Model** the Way of the Guardian

The Deep-Training Approach

We are creatures of habit and pattern, so how we play a game dictates how we perform on a Mission. This is a crucial point because when we are in the heat of a Mission, we often have to act quickly. There is no time to assess and choose options. We need to rely on the instinctive responses we learned in training.

Developing a learned ability requires the creation of new neural synapses in the brain. The process is accomplished through consistent repetition. Without repetition, we automatically resort to our previous ineffective behaviors. This creates continued poor performance, which strengthens the old synapses that lock us into performing poorly. Without constant use, the new synapses we strive to create weaken and eventually fade altogether.

We can circumvent that dilemma by following the Guardian precept that *Training is life, and life is training.* In other words, the dedicated Guardian is always in training, even after she has completed the formal instruction. Part III of this book offers training exercises that fit into your regular routine and require little extra time or energy. With most of the exercises incorporating stealth training, the people around you won't notice anything out of the ordinary. They may even become your training coaches, as you need to secretly perform in their presence. *Training is life, and life is training* is at the core of the on-the-ground trainings I run. I seldom tell the Trainees whether we are carrying out an actual Mission or just conducting an exercise. In this way, they learn to always be Mission-ready and perform at their peak.

The Guardian as Healer

An essential component of Guardian Training is healing the psycho-emotional wounds that keep us in a defensive, self-serving mode. In such a state, it is virtually impossible for us to have the perspective and wherewithal to play to visibly lose, while at the same time playing to win the underlying objective, which is to serve the Greater Good.

Let me be clear that The Guardian trains hard to win; and on a Mission, he gives himself no option other than winning—but never for himself.

Most other people play win-or-lose, which is focused on getting the most points, recognition, or personal gain. Board games, sports, politics, employment, nationalism—even religion and dating—are win-lose propositions.

The difference between the two approaches is monumental. If we as a species keep playing this reckless win-lose game with our lives and our world, we will accomplish nothing less than fulfilling an epic death wish, for both our species and our Mother Planet. On the other hand, when we create win-wins, we turn the tide from combativeness to nurturance and healing.

Why, then, are so many people totally committed to the win-lose model? Of the numerous replies I've received, nearly all of them boil down to this: The great majority of our population are victims of trauma. Sufferers of sexual assault or returning military personnel who struggle with Post-Traumatic Stress Disorder (PTSD) typically come to mind when we think of traumatized people.

However, for most of us, traumatization occurs much earlier. We may have been deeply wounded at birth or shortly thereafter. If we were isolated in cribs and not adequately held or breastfed, we likely suffered separation anxiety: a precursor to trauma. Oppressive parenting practices, bullying, a dehumanizing educational system, and domestic violence are other common trauma causes.

Trauma automatically turns on self-preservation mode, which activates the fight-flight response. The *fight* component tends to make people aggressive, and the *flight* component makes them defensive. In order to serve the Greater Good, the Guardian needs to be free of both aggressive and defensive tendencies.

Healing the Trauma That Haunts Us could serve as another subtitle for this book. Along with tending to her people's torments, the quintessential Guardian addresses the underlying traumas causing them. In traditional cultures, a Guardian is continually on the lookout for struggling individuals and hurtful behaviors. Through example and guidance, a Guardian works to restore mindfulness and compassion within her community and helps its members move on from their painful pasts.

Guardian Training itself is therapeutic. It provides methods and a supportive environment for traumatized people to manage their *Trauma Memory Responses* (TMRs), which are the residual reactions they experience after traumatic experiences. Because the Training requires a tremendous amount of self-reflection, it allows people to consider potential lessons gleaned from a traumatic experience and put them to good use.

Finding Trust

Through the Training, I've watched a number of traumatized individuals learn how to trust again. In doing so, they have been able to become valued Protectors of their people. (For more on this topic, see my book Breaking the Trauma Code.)

Time to Choose

Picture yourself being challenged in ways you cannot even imagine. The unknown unleashes a deep fear for your safety, yet you step into it—because you know in your heart that you have no other choice. For you, there is only one life: dancing out on the edge of what you think is possible, in order to fulfill your destiny and be of service to your community.

Is this you? Do you want to become who you are intended to be—the best possible version of yourself?

If you do not have clear answers to these questions, our time together may be over for now. It's possible that you have not yet experienced the calling to be a Guardian, or that the wounds from struggling with modern life are clouding your vision of yourself. Whatever the case, I suggest that you lay this book down, at least for now. More words only bring more confusion to matters of the heart. Besides, my intent is not to talk anyone into anything, but only to serve those who feel ready.

With Native People, there are no *goodbyes*. When the Ojibwe Indians of Northern Wisconsin part company, they say "*Giga-wabaman*," which means *You will continue to be seen by me*. If at some point you choose to move forward with Guardian Training, I would consider it an honor to be your guide.

On the other hand, if you now feel a deep yearning for what my words convey—the deep satisfaction of those who dedicate their lives to service and the quest for Truth—stay with me. Together we will embark on this sacred, high adventure out beyond what we think we know and what we believe is possible.

CHAPTER 3

LIKE A WOLF: THE THREE ARCHETYPES

In order to explore the ways Guardians function, we need context. Whether we're considering Wolves, Lions, or nearly any other social animal—including us Humans—each of us belongs to one of three archetypes. In our *packs*, prides, clans, and other social units, we each play one of three archetypal roles:

Nurturer

- Tends to the welfare of the pups, acting as babysitter, playmate, healthcare provider, and Protector
- Cares for any sick or injured packmates

Voice

- The pack's galvanizer and point person
- Synthesizes information, then directs the pack's course of action
- Speaks and negotiates for the pack
- In the center of most activities

Guardian

- Acts as lookout, guard, information gatherer, spy, message bearer, Protector, and Scout
- Relays important observations back to the rest of the pack
- Holds to the periphery

Nurturers, *Voices*, and Guardians work together like the fingers on a hand to create a strong grip, gentle touch, and wise direction-pointing. Almost entirely by instinct, the fingers can move synchronously as one and communicate instantly without a sound. Each of us is genetically programmed to fill one of the archetypal roles and work simultaneously with the other arche-types, like interdependent fingers.

At the same time, it's not always clear that one person is a Nurturer, the next is a Voice, and the one over there is a Guardian. The instruction I received from the Elders clarifies that even though we predominantly identify with one arche-type, we all have some of the other two archetypes within us. In the *Old Days*, people would develop the skills of all three archetypes so that they could serve their people in whatever way was necessary.

The Elders said that the degree of prominence of one arche-type over another varies from individual to individual. Occasion-ally a person comes along who is strong in two archetypes, and there is the rare person who has an even Balance of all three (see chart).

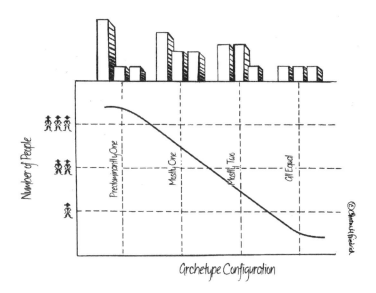

Chart 1: Number of People in Each Archetype

This lends diversity to the clan or pack and allows individuals to serve in multiple roles, as needed. If Nurturer is my predominant archetype, I feel best caring for the children and the hearth because it's what I'm designed to do. However, when Guardians are needed, I like stepping forth to serve in that role as well. I have some innate Guardian ability, and I have trained with the Guardians. The same is true for the Voice role: If someone is needed to speak for the clan, I can do it, even though it may not be my main strength.

It's All about Relationship

In order to fully understand the archetypes, we need to understand each of their roles in the pack. In a pack formation, we have a Voice or Voice pair up front, a Tail (who may be either a Nurturer or a Guardian) bringing up the rear, and everyone else in the middle. The Nurturers usually surround the younger or weaker members of the group, and the Guardians typically stay on the sides or bring up the rear.

The communication between the Voice and the Tail is important because they each see a different slice of their environment. If everything is alright ahead of and behind the pack, it's likely that they're in good shape. The Voice and the Tail also determine the speed of the group. They choose a speed that will accommodate everyone. If something happens to a member in the middle of the group, the Tail alerts the Voice to slow down so that everyone can stay together and figure out their next move.

If the group believes the Voice has made an error, then it is up to the rest of the group to engage in non-verbal communication. Not all communication can be non-verbal, but there are simple cues for stop, go, and slow down, for example. If the Voice has made a mistake, the group members can at first signal to each other, then say something directly to the Voice. This communication may take the form of an audible cue, like rustling a branch or making an animal sound. The idea is to establish a set of cues among the group so they can understand one another even when their goal is to stay invisible and silent.

We can better understand the Guardian archetype, as well as the other main archetypes, Voice and Nurturer, by looking at how the pack is structured and its relationship to place. Nearly every pack of Wolves is built upon what is typically referred to as *alpha pair.* They produce the pups, and first- and second-generation pups generally comprise the rest of the pack. Occasionally an alien Wolf is allowed to join, but most often he hovers around the pack's periphery. Packs generally run from five to fifteen animals.

When Wolf country is in a stable state, every pack has a territory. When a pack abandons its territory because of an environmental disaster, competition from another pack, or insufficient prey, it immediately seeks another territory. The territory defines the pack more so than the animals in the pack. Individuals can—and will—come and go. However, the den and rendezvous sites, along with territorial boundaries and established trails, are essential to the pack's well-being and define its personality.

Territory size is determined by:

- Pack size
- Size of prey base
- Pressure from surrounding packs
- What is needed to establish and maintain a sense of security and comfort

Conflict between Packs

There is seldom only one pack in an area, and packs in a given area are seldom of equal size. Nor do they have equal needs or an equal prey base. In addition, topography varies from territory to territory, which creates variations in movement patterns, hunting techniques, and prey survival. All of this creates a fluid dynamic among the packs in a particular region, as they work out how to best meet their needs without infringing upon those of their neighbors. Imagine looking down upon a mosaic of territories that are slowly—yet continually—in flux. Boundaries meander one way, then another. Some territories grow a little larger and some a little smaller, and occasionally one gets absorbed by another.

Now picture a pack with six pups who survive to adolescence, which is an unusually large number. They are three-quarters grown, and they have begun to hunt with the pack. In one short season, the pack size has doubled, as has the number of mouths to feed. All of a sudden, there aren't enough Deer to feed them all.

Another factor comes into play: The pups' lives have expanded beyond the den. When the pups stayed close to the den, the pack brought food to them, and pack life centered on the den. Now that the pups are mobile, the kill site is the feasting and socializing location. A number of loafing and rendezvous sites are utilized while hunting and patrolling territorial boundaries. This increased activity puts pressure on those boundaries, which means the pack needs to either expand its territory or find a new one.

Predators are designed to be lazy. When they have full bellies and no stress, they like to lie around and nap. This is an evolved survival strategy that gives them the opportunity to digest food (usually eaten in large quantities after a kill), unwind, and physically recuperate. Well-fed predators have no motivation to expand their territories—or to defend against minor incursions. However, this pack is restless. It is not making enough kills to sustain itself, and it has to start hunting outside of its territory.

The pack sets out on its journey. It quickly hits another territory. The boundary is established with scent posts marked by urine. The pack members were already feeling anxious when they started venturing away from their home territory, and now after picking up the scent of the alien neighbors, they are on high alert.

Within each of them, two opposing forces rage: hunger and anxiety. One drives them out of their territory and the other strives to keep them there. No animal likes to be stressed, yet this is the present reality and adjustments need to be made. It is a matter of survival.

The Meeting

The closer the pack gets to the edge of its territory, the more its members come together and fall into formation. The alpha pair, who are the pack's Voices, are up front. The pups are in the center, surrounded by their aunts and uncles, who serve as Nurturers. The Guardians scout ahead and watch the flanks and rear, so that they can pick up on any surprises.

The Guardians, determined to meet the needs of the pack, are ready for any contingency. In following the Guardian Way, they have prepared themselves for the worst-case scenario. Even though the scent posts were not marked recently and there is no other sign of the neighboring pack in the area, they cannot afford to take any chances. Their pups are their future, and they rely on the other members of the pack as intensely as you rely on your heart and lungs. The other pack—or any other challenge—could show up out of the blue, and they are ready for it.

The pack crosses the boundary. To the pack, this action is motivated by a sincere need to feed its young. To the neighboring pack, it is an invasion. It doesn't take long for the ripple effect to bring the news of a major disturbance to the home pack, and they silently speed toward the source.

The two packs sense each other's presence before they come in sight of each other, and the forward Guardians soon confirm it. Our pack, on new and unfamiliar territory, takes a defensive position, with its Voices up front to direct and make decisions. Without losing focus on the threat, the front pair remains acutely keyed in to the Guardians. Like set traps, the Guardians are ready to shift position or rush in the instant they are needed. What matters most to all is the safety of the pups— the pack's future. The calm, stable presence of the Nurturers keeps the Wolflings quiet and contained.

The home pack switches to offensive mode, with Guardians in the front line. It looks ominous, yet at the same time nobody wants to fight. Invader or defender, the cost is the same. Injured pack members are a liability, and the loss of any pack members can result in fewer successful hunts. The smaller a pack gets, the more susceptible its territory is to takeover.

The much-preferred option is negotiation, which is carried out by the Voices. Tentatively at first, yet with pomp and circumstance—raised tails, flared hackles, and high on the toes— the Voice pairs approach each other. With enough rumble deep in their throats to show they mean business, but not enough to trigger an attack, they suspiciously eye each other.

The posturing gets more intense, more assertive. Whenever one of them nearly crosses the boundary of this ritual sizing-up, his counterpart launches a bluff attack to reestablish protocol. With hackles raised, teeth bared, and thunder rumbling from their pulsing chests, the Voices represent their packs by taking commanding positions to defend them.

While this is happening, Guardians on both sides scout out the other pack, to see how numerous and strong they are. This behavior is also seen with Lions, who wander at night. A pride can tell the size of a new pride moving into its territory by listening to its growls. If the new pride is bigger than them, the home pride just melts away without conflict. The same is true when the home pride is larger or stronger—the new pride retreats without a confrontation. Like Wolves, Lions have no love for fighting.

Back to our packs: They're going to take the path of least resistance. To their opponents, our pack looks strong; their ranks are inflated by six nearly grown pups. And they all look hungry, which they show with the intensity of their presence.

The home pack is just over half the size of the invaders, yet they have much at stake. If they lose this territory, it will be a long time before they can find new land and a new food source. Even though their Guardians shoot questioning looks at those who are ready to defend, they find it impossible to retreat. In a flash, a scuffle breaks out. Only the Voices and a few Guardians jump in. The Nurturers stay back to protect the pups if needed.

Right away it becomes apparent to the home pack that they will be torn to shreds if they try to drive off the intruders. The smaller group backs off, yet maintains its integrity by standing tall and baring their teeth. The message is clear: You have established your presence here, but if you dare to venture any farther than necessary in order to meet your needs, you better watch your backsides.

View your culture through the window of this story. Every nuance of our social, political, and familial relations is represented, as well as the roles we each play in those relations. I was thus able to take what I learned from living with Wolves and apply it directly to my interactions with Humans. That includes what I learned from the Wolves about the Guardian Way. Much of what I share is merely giving words to what they taught me.

CHAPTER 4

DETERMINE YOUR ARCHETYPE

Which role did you relate to the most in the previous chapter's story: Voice, Nurturer, or Guardian? We'll explore that question more deeply in a moment; first, let's take a closer look at the duties the Guardians performed. The Guardians of the pack served as the Scouts, tasked with sharing relevant information with the rest of the group, and also as the guards, prepared for anything that might happen. The rest of both packs took their cues from the Guardians. Through it all, the Guardians remained calm and unassuming. Instead of attacking outright, they watched—some inconspicuously—to see what would unfold naturally.

In order to best advise the rest of the pack, they intuitively tuned into what both their pack and the other pack were feeling. Largely because of the Guardians' sharp senses and perceptive abilities, the packs were able to serve the Greater Good by meeting and departing without conflict.

If you identified most with the role of the Guardian, consider Guardian Training. Developing your skills as a Guardian will help you reach your full potential in order to best be of service to your people and our Earth Mother.

Some people struggle to identify with an archetype, even though the archetypes may appear to be clear in the story. These people wonder if Guardian Training is right for them, or whether it might be better to develop their nurturing side or their leadership abilities. I recommend the following three ways to help get in touch with your inner calling:

1. Look at your life.

Check the questions in each group that apply to you.

Group 1

- Are you a *natural* caretaker who feels protective of your friends and family?
- Do you love tending plants or growing your own food?
- Do you feel confident providing emotional comfort to your loved ones?
- Are you empathetic and relate easily to others?
- Do you love children and marvel at how they see the world?

Group 2

- Do you enjoy stepping up and taking charge, such as organizing an event?
- Do you typically hold positions of authority?
- Are you often the decision maker in your relationships?
- Are you comfortable speaking in front of people?
- Are you often looked to for advice?

Group 3

- Do you like to find pieces that others have missed when solving problems?
- Are you often the one to suggest adventures and new places to explore?
- Are you naturally inquisitive?
- Are you highly sensitive and in tune to the actions and reactions of others?
- Do you notice things that many people do not?

If most or all of the questions in Group 1 apply to you, it's likely that your archetype is Nurturer. If you identify with the majority of the questions in Group 2, you are probably a Voice. If Group 3's questions most resonate with you, odds are you're a Guardian.

The majority of people find the bulk of their checked questions in one grouping, so it is clear which archetype they are. Some find themselves relating to two archetypes, and a few have roots in all three. The latter make good generalists, able to serve wherever needed.

In some traditional cultures, young people train in each of the archetypal roles, no matter what their specific predisposition. Then, when necessary, they can fill in wherever needed.

2. Role-play.

Reflect on notable roles you have played. Over the past day, what characteristics have you exhibited in group situations? Ask for help from family members and close friends. Yet clarity often comes from within, especially when noting the roles we play in our dreams.

Another approach: Close your eyes and go back to the Wolf story. Become a member of the pack. Where do you feel most comfortable? Are you in the middle taking care of the pups, or are you up front, at the apex of all the action? Maybe you are drifting in the shadows, watching and gathering information.

Remember that you can feel comfortable with more than one role. Even if a couple of roles fit, one will probably be a little more formfitting than the other. *Feel* while you're role-playing. Do you experience a deep sense of calm when you imagine yourself occupying one of the roles? Does your heart start beating faster with anxiety when you imagine another? Tune in to your body's responses, both emotional and physical.

3. Reflect on how you handle stress.

The ways in which we handle stressful or threatening situations is an accurate indicator of our archetype. In order to read the indicator properly, we need to understand the inaccuracy of the commonly used concept of the *fight-flight-freeze response*. Behaviorists have categorized the range of reactions to perceived harm into *fight, flight,* and *freeze*. After living with both wild and domestic animals for many years, I have found this categorization to be incomplete and reflecting cultural bias.

We attach a high value to Voice behavior, as exhibited by prominent political, religious, and sports figures, and males as heads of family. Correspondingly, we either ignore or give second-class status to Nurturers (housewives, nurses, and other human service providers) and Guardians (military, police, fire and rescue personnel). From this cultural lens, the threat-response options clearly appear to be fight-flight-freeze; police and the military typically fight, and housewives and nurses flee or freeze.

However, a Guardian's response protocol is to first scout and observe, while a Nurturer assesses core needs and a Voice listens, processes input, and directs a course of action. These tendencies lead to different threat responses, which become apparent only when we immerse ourselves in each archetypal role. Here is a more complete picture, as I have learned it:

- **Voice response** = fight or flight
- **Nurturer response** = gather together or tend
- **Guardian response** = fade or blend

This leaves the nagging issue of the *freeze response*. Again, using this term shows a lack of understanding regarding what is really occurring. Animals only appear to be freezing to those who fail to recognize what they *are* doing. A stationary animal under imminent threat is anything but frozen. There is a flurry of activity that we can identify by reliving one of the times that we "froze up" when overwhelmed.

In the Wolf story, we saw examples of each of the three stress responses. Take a moment to think about how you respond to stress in your daily life. You respond in one or more of those fundamental ways, even though it may not be obvious. When you're with a group of people and there is tension, do you wish you could just disappear like a Guardian? Do you try to fix things and make everyone feel comfortable, as a Nurturer would? Or do you want to take action and either stand up for someone's rights or get personally involved in the argument, which is consistent with the Voice archetype?

To reveal your response pattern, recall a few uncomfortable and threatening situations from your past and how you responded. Whatever the situations, the odds are that you responded similarly most of the time.

False Readings

If you felt innately comfortable with the role or roles these exercises identified for you, it's a solid indication that you are in touch with your innate archetypal self and it is manifesting in your life. However, if you were emotionally triggered by the exercises, or if they left you feeling apathetic, it is possible that some of the scripts you play out in your life are not the real you.

Even though you have a natural inclination to respond according to your archetype, other factors can either mask it or cause you to react as though you were of another archetype. The most common factors are cultural and family conditioning, behavioral patterns adopted to survive high-stress situations, and personality changes resulting from trauma.

A Nurturer who was continually exploited as a child may have learned to respond aggressively to her environment as a survival mechanism. She carried this behavior into adulthood, which now causes her to appear as a Voice, even though her true Nature is still that of a Nurturer. Another child learned to endure abuse by fading into the background, so he now passes as a Guardian.

The way to determine your authentic response is not by what you do (which is your patterned behavior and is influenced by outside factors), but by your first impulse. What did you immediately *feel* like doing before you switched gears and went with your patterned behavior? This initial urge is what indicates your true archetype.

Even though you may have learned to function in this new role, you will never feel completely at ease in it. There will always be some level of unwelcome stress (in extreme cases, even resentment or dread) followed by a sense of relief after the present task demanded by the role is over.

If you are getting false readings, I encourage you to examine the behavioral patterns that keep you suppressed. When you break free from these constraints, you will embark on your Journey of Self-Discovery. You owe it to both yourself and your people.

CHAPTER 5

THE ROLES OF THE TRADITIONAL GUARDIAN

"Spear an Indian, save a Walleye!"
"Timber Nigger!"
"Hey Geronimo, get a job!"

The raucous rabble closed in on us, and we suddenly realized that we were surrounded. We didn't have to see the beer cans and whiskey bottles; we could smell their inspiration on the crowd's collective breath. They pushed a barrage of signs echoing their epithets into our faces, which forced us to huddle tighter and tighter around the boat landing. Even though a stone or beer can or wad of spit might have come flying our way, we dared not react, lest we detonate the bomb that engulfed us.

We were about two dozen Natives exercising our newly reestablished treaty right to spear Fish during the spring spawning season, along with an equal number of non-Native supporters. They were more than 200 Northwoods sportsmen and women who came to protest our fishing. Six of our spearers had just gone out in their boats after a ceremony honoring the spirit of the Fish and a smudging of the spearers and their equipment. Around their dinghies whirled the speedboats of protesters, who were trying to create waves big enough to swamp the spearers.

Sandwiched between the water and the seething crowd, we supporters had no option but to maintain our presence. We did so by standing tall and yet appearing non-threatening. Without making eye contact, without responding to the harassment, we stood our ground. We did not speak a word, either amongst ourselves or to our tormentors. Our intent was to give them no indication that we were intimidated, nor any incentive to escalate their threats. Each of us was painfully aware that the least ripple in this tenuous standoff could result in us being literally trampled.

Just when the tension was ready to snap, we heard a calming sound come drifting over the din. Faintly at first, then louder and louder, came the drumming and chanting. Was it an illusion? A desperate attempt to find strength and focus in the face of crisis?

The sounds came closer and grew more real. All heads turned, and the swaggering mob calmed to a murmur and stared open-mouthed. Six chanters circled a large Drum they were playing, and they were followed by two dozen or so women and Elders. The procession wove through the crowd as though it did not exist. They walked straight and dignified, but without arrogance. No eye contact or other gesture of recognition of the throng around them was made. They could just as well have been walking through a tranquil meadow, with only the wildflowers to hear their song.

When they reached us, we joined in their chant. Not defiantly, not boisterously, but in the spirit of a people who belong and who will walk their given Path in serenity and purpose, no matter what the adversity.

We continued until the spearers came off the water. Along with the drummers and chanters, we then led them out through the crowd and away from the landing without incident.

The story I just shared with you occurred in the early spring of 1988. I was serving as an *Ogichida*, which is the term for Guardian Warrior in the language of the Ojibwe Elders who trained me when I was a young adult. I was given the designation by the Ojibwe for serving beside them in the 1987-1991 Wisconsin Walleye War. It erupted when sports fishermen and resort owners clashed with the members of six Northern Wisconsin Ojibwe tribes who were exercising their newly reaffirmed treaty right to spearfish Walleye during the early-spring spawning season.

In a 1975 court case, the tribes challenged efforts by the state of Wisconsin to regulate their off-reservation hunting and fishing rights, which were guaranteed in the 1837 St. Peters Treaty and the 1842 La Pointe Treaty. The Walleye War erupted immediately after U.S. District Court Judge Barbara Crabb's August 21, 1987 ruling that the six tribes retained the right under these treaties to hunt and fish throughout their former territory.

The Walleye War ended in 1991, after the Ogichida and other tribal supporters successfully petitioned federal courts to issue an injunction against the protesters.

Rooted in Tradition

The Guardian possesses characteristic traits, which equip her to be entrusted with specific roles in serving her people. My Guardian kin and I enacted a number of those roles during the Walleye War. We will explore the Training and maturation of the Guardian in indigenous cultures in order to draw inspiration for our Training and maturation.

First, let's take a look at the Guardian Way through the lens of a traditional culture. My formal Training started at around age seven, when my father invited a Menominee Elder to join us for an evening meal. Being fascinated with anything "Indian" as early as I can remember, I peppered him with questions on hunting, scouting, growing up Indian, living in a wigwam, and anything else that came to mind.

After about fifteen minutes, my dad politely—yet clearly—asked if I could slow up a bit to give the man a chance to eat. Undoubtedly blushing out of *self-consciousness*, I found my silence and went back to eating as well.

Yet the Elder and I kept talking, only nobody else knew. Having been raised as much by the wildlings in the woods and swamps outside our door as by my parents, I knew and spoke the spontaneous, intuitive language of all things wild. Without missing a beat, the Elder switched to what I now call *Nature-speak*, and we kept our conversation going.

Right there at the dinner table, I received lessons in stealth, deception, and service to the Greater Good, while at the same time honoring the ways of my people. That was the beginning of my formal Training as an Ogichida.

Some related Ojibwe terms help reveal the soul of the Ogichida Gichitwa[1], which refers to *someone who puts the cares and concerns of others before himself* and may be the root term from which *Ogichida* originated. He is highly regarded by his people because when he is asked, he steps out front to take care of his relatives, his clan, and his nation. He looks after the language and ceremonies, tends to the health and general welfare of the people, and advocates for their civil rights.

Manaajiidiwin, a term used in reference to the Ogichida, means *to be respectful and go easy on each other.* Rather than respect for those with status or in positions of authority, as is practiced in our culture, respect of the Manaajiidiwin type means to treat others with great care, concern, and affection. There is mutual trust and support. Rather than criticizing, they listen deeply to each other and honor each other's Truths; and instead of gossiping, they speak directly to each other.

Young Ogichida (from the age of around twenty to forty) who contribute whatever they hunt, fish, or trap to those in need are referred to as *Kizhenaabeg*, which means *the benevolent Humans.* As they mature further, they often become the leaders of their people.

Service Roles

The traditional Guardian serves as emissary and scout, Protector and provider, healer and advisor, mediator and mentor.

She is sent to councils, feasts, and ceremonies to represent her people (and sometimes a particular individual). Because of her Training, which takes her beyond herself and into the consciousness of her people, she is trusted by them to represent, speak, and negotiate for them. They know that she will speak for them honorably and accurately.

When her people are on the move, she scouts ahead of them to assure their safe passage by locating the best trails and making arrangements with the people whose land they are passing through. She will probably not lead directly, but more through clear yet well-disguised signs that she leaves in her wake.

She sets up trade and skill-exchange meetings, always with the additional goal of fostering friendship. Ever courteous as a guest, she listens to her peers from other tribes, then objectively and concisely transmits to her people what she observed and was given to bring back to them. Her hosts know her qualities and trust in her words, because they know that every Guardian, no matter of what people, upholds the honor of all people and expresses herself with the integrity of a Truth-speaker.

A master of the skills of stealth, observation, and tracking, she is relied upon to gather useful information outside of her people's normal realm of functioning. She finds the locations of needed plants, animals, and craft materials, and she is trained to detect anything out of the ordinary, whether it be environmental or people-related. She watches over the children and the general health of her people, and she keeps the Elders and others informed of anything that will help them better serve the people in the ways that they are called.

The Guardian as Motion

The traditional Guardian learns early on that movement lies at the core of his ability to serve. In the story that opened this chapter, everything the Guardians thought or acted upon was movement-oriented. The Guardian chooses to speak more through action than words, and his Training and service are manifest in action.

In Guardian-honoring cultures, training begins at an early age. Even before he can walk, he is instructed in the core skills of the Scout, one of which is to become silent when necessary. This means arresting his talking or crying when he is given the signal.

Some of the early training, such as the example I just gave, could appear harsh to those of us living the Civilized Way, as it seems to stretch the capabilities of a child. We may perceive early training this way because our innate abilities have been squelched or have atrophied to the extent that we have forgotten about them. The Truth is that we have tremendous unrecognized and untapped physical strength and stamina, intuitive and awareness abilities, and intellectual capacities, even as children.

One reason we don't recognize it is that we tend to focus on and develop a single ability at a time. However, our abilities are designed to be mutually supportive and magnify each other. So if we do not develop as a whole being, but only seek to hone a certain attribute, even that attribute will not develop to its full potential. What we often interpret as the tremendous and almost unrealistic feats of the Guardian are actually quite within his—and all of our—normal ranges of experience and ability.

The Guardian-in-training learns to move undetected. He does not rely upon camouflage or becoming invisible, because camouflage can fail and what is invisible in one moment can be visible in the next. These are techniques employed and relied upon by Civilized People because they are not at one with their *Circle of Life*, so they must either camouflage themselves to appear that they are, or become invisible to create the illusion that they are not even there.

The Native Guardian, on the other hand, moves within the greater movement. He is like the tree who bends in unison with his sister trees when the Wind asks them to bend, and stands unflinching with them when the Wind is quiet beyond a whisper. Although he is fully visible along with the other trees, he draws no more attention and creates no more disturbance than any one tree among the thousands rustling and swaying in unison.

As with his non-Human kin, the Guardian will sometimes use camouflage or invisibility, but only as an adjunct, and minimally at that, rather than relying upon it. Because he is a fully functioning and integrated child of the Earth, he already fits into his environment. He smells like his surroundings because he eats, drinks, and grooms with the natural resources the Mother gives him. His clothing and accouterments blend in with his surroundings because they are *of* his surroundings.

Rather than being ego-centered and seeing himself as distinct from the natural realm, and therefore standing out, his consciousness operates in unison with the greater consciousness of his Life Circle. He then blends so seamlessly with his environment that he could appear to be invisible. He is like the Wolf who travels with the Caribou and has no need to be invisible. When Wolf moves in sync with Caribou's movement, she raises no alarm. Only when Wolf grows hungry, and thus begins to move differently, do the Caribou notice her and react.

As much as Wolf and our plant and animal kin know how to move instinctively in this way, so do we. Only we have forced ourselves to move by the clock rather than the Caribou, and bend to the commands of others rather than the touch of the Wind, which has squelched our instincts in favor of bending to the will of others.

One of our innate movement abilities is tracking, and we are designed to be masters at it. The renowned tracking feats of the Native Guardian are commonly exhibited by many, rather than being rare and phenomenal accomplishments. The Native hears the *song of the track,* which is comprised of a chorus of voices that carry on a conversation about who passed by, and when and why.

These voices are not speaking to her as much as she is eavesdropping on the going gossip. She knows the impulses of the one she is tracking—his hungers and fears and drives. This enables her to move within his movement. She is often aware of where he is going, so she can speed ahead of him and wait for his arrival. This ability of the Native Guardian transcends that of the typical tracker, as the Guardian is no more consciously following a trail than you would be if you were going to meet a friend at a park. Having a good hunch where your friend will be in the park, you can go directly there rather than needing to retrace her footsteps. (My book, *Entering the Mind of the Tracker: Native Practices for Developing Intuitive Consciousness and Discovering Hidden Nature*, takes you deep into the world of animals and the mysteries of your innate abilities.)

In recognition of the profound role stories play in the development of the Guardian, I started this chapter with a story. In a traditional training camp, it would be the Elder Guardians around the evening hearthfire recounting the adventures of their younger days. Yet you can benefit in the same way, by having videos and books on the Guardian Way be your storytellers. There you will meet Elders, Guardians, and Guardian Animals, who will take you beyond your present reality and inspire you to perform in ways that you innately knew—but never *thought*—you were capable of.

Chapter 5 Citations

1   For more on this term and the following two Ojibwe terms, see James Vukelich (Kaagegaabaw), Turtle clan, at www.jamesvukelich.com.

CHAPTER 6

THE GUARDIAN WAY TODAY

We've been talking about the Guardian's primary role of serving his people rather than focusing on just himself and his immediate family. Yet when he serves others, it turns out that he serves himself more than if he were to act selfishly. When he keeps his people at the forefront, they grow stronger and are ever more willing and able to help him in return. Everyone benefits more than if each person was primarily self-focused.

I learned from the Elders this basic teaching: *Giving is receiving.* They told me that you don't ask yourself, "What's in it for me?" or "What can I gain here?" Instead, you take care of your people first, and then you receive your people's support and trust. Because you have devoted your time to strengthening relationships with your people, they are going to be there to serve and support you when you need it. This emphasis on servitude is the cornerstone of the Guardian Way.

But it's not just serving, the Elders said; it's *how* you serve. You must be dispassionate, without emotion or feeling. If you approach a situation with an emotional charge, or if you are looking for emotional satisfaction, you will not be able to maintain a consistent level of perspective and centeredness.

Instead, set your feelings aside and focus on being fully present. In the end, feelings come and go; whether someone in need is served or not is the truly important thing. Serving dispassionately is how you establish relationships with your people and yourself.

Sometimes Guardians serve others in ways that are not immediately recognizable. For example, at mealtime in a Native village, the Elders are served first. If there is a shortage of food, they are assured the necessary sustenance to continue as the knowledge holders and intergenerational bridge to keep the clan viable. Next to be served are pregnant and nursing women, followed by non-childbearing women, then the males of the clan who serve as Voices and Nurturers.

The last to eat are the Guardians, because if there is not enough food, they have the highest level of physical fitness and can most easily go without. Also, they are best able to forage something for themselves.

Missions: The Guardian's Heartbeat

Special services that a Guardian performs to train herself and strengthen her community are called Missions. When dominant forces run contrary to honor and respect for all life, Missions often need to be covert. As much as possible, Guardians conduct their Missions in the open, to involve as many stakeholders as possible. They provide valuable energy and support, and the Mission itself is an example and teacher for others in the community.

Missions are essential to Guardian Training because they involve several key abilities such as physical and mental conditioning, breaking patterns, planning, stealth, scouting, and *signaling*. To the Guardian, there is no difference between Training and Service Missions. In fact, she is often not informed of which it is, so that she learns to dedicate her whole being to whatever she does. Hence the Guardian maxim: *Life is training, and training is life.*

Missions Then and Now

In this day of complex societal structures and a bewildering array of threats to Mother Earth and her children, Missions can take on a character that makes them seem unrecognizable when compared with the Missions of old. Yet the core of all Missions–and the motivation for performing them–is the same as it has always been.

Now we take a look at the basic components of a Mission, then build upon them as we progress through the Training. A Mission starts with planning, which is a precise science. As much as possible needs to be orchestrated before the Mission begins because it's easier to complete any task when you are rested, relaxed, and know what to expect. Solid preparation reduces delays and distractions and makes a Mission more likely to succeed.

If an unknown variable arises during the Mission and the pack has the underpinning of a solid plan, the issue can usually be resolved quickly and efficiently. The main focus areas for Mission planning are:

- Pre-planning reconnaissance
- Directions and alternative directions to the Mission site
- A Mission diagram
- Escape routes and cover stories, in case the Mission needs to be aborted
- Expected weather, human activity, and any other variables that might arise
- Timelines for all Mission components
- Rendezvous sites and precise times, for staging, regrouping, and rest
- Post-Mission debriefing plans for as soon after Mission completion as possible

With those parameters in place, decision-making is facilitated, unknown variables are greatly reduced, and the odds of Mission success are high.

Rendezvous sites are a key and often overlooked component of Mission planning. It does not matter whether it is a solo or pack Mission, or whether it is conducted covertly or overtly. A rendezvous offers the time and space to assess progress, regain perspective, and recharge. Knowing a rendezvous is coming up can give a stressed or weary pack member the extra charge needed to keep going. Perhaps most importantly, rendezvous reinforce Pack Consciousness and engage the entire pack in any implementation adjustments that need to be made.

Mission Priorities

To help bring to light the deep motivations that draw us to a Mission, I'll use the metaphor of a Wolf pack preparing for a hunt. Their main motivation is to feed the pups—the future of the pack. When the howl goes out, all pack members stop what they're doing and proceed posthaste to their rendezvous site.

They don't hesitate. They may not know why the rendezvous howl was raised, but they *do* know that the one who raised the howl did it for the good of the pack. The howl could signify a Bear is attacking the den or the appearance of an invading pack. Whatever the reason, they know that for the common good they must congregate quickly.

The pack has predetermined rendezvous sites, so they know where to meet in order to help each other in the event of injury or attack. A rendezvous-centered Mission keeps the pack functioning in a seamless, nonverbal flow in times of extreme challenge or disarray.

Pack Trust

Each pack member knows that her needs will be taken care of within the context of the pack, rather than her having to leave the pack in order to take care of herself. This gives her and each of her packmates the core motivation to always put the needs of the pack first.

The pack-first approach necessitates that the main underlying priority of Mission members is to remain unseen. The less exposure, the less risk. On an overt Mission, invisibility helps keep the focus on the purpose rather than the orchestrators; and on a covert Mission, invisibility is a matter of personal safety and Mission success. For these reasons, *all Missions are—at least to some degree—stealth Missions.*

After the Mission, the pack—whether Wolf or Human—conducts a debriefing. The members discuss what worked, what didn't work, and what could be improved for the next Mission. Each individual thinks about his or her personal contributions during the Mission and any changes for next time that might serve the pack. The pack also addresses what could be done to better serve each individual. Along with improving the next Mission, the debriefing strengthens the pack as a whole.

The Guardian Intensive Trainings I run at the Teaching Drum Outdoor School are centered around the daily planning and completion of Missions, both pack and solo. It might be gathering food, finding water, tracking an animal, exploring a new territory, or executing a clandestine operation. My Guardian At-Home Trainings can also include Missions.

To Become a Fully Functioning Guardian

There are no limits in the Guardian Way. The Guardian is capable of being anything he wants to be and assuming a wide variety of roles in order to meet the needs of his community. Here is the four-step approach he takes for achieving that boundless state:

1. **Dedicate yourself to a training program.** You may create one of your own, use the one presented in this book, or find another one that fits for you.

2. **Develop sensory acuity.** A pack needs to move efficiently and silently, which requires a high level of sensory attunement. The exercises in Part IV of my book, *Journey to the Ancestral Self,* are designed specifically for this purpose.

3. **Improve your communication skills.** They are crucial for functioning with a single mind and purpose, like the fingers on a hand. To learn the Native Way of clear, quick, and precise communication, I recommend my book *Truthspeaking: Ancestral Ways to Hear and Speak the Voice of the Heart.*

4. **Convert to the Guardian Diet.** We are what we eat, which is especially true for us Guardians, who need optimal nutritional support to function at our peak. Research continually shows that we are stronger, faster, more intelligent, healthier, and enjoy longer lives on a *Guardian Diet* (see Chapter 14).

Serving in Everyday Life

A reaction I sometimes get to the idea of Guardian Training is, "What use is it?" Some think the Guardian Way is a relic from the past; which is where it ought to stay. Others see it as mythology, which has entertainment value and that's about it. Still others see value in it for personal development and an adrenaline rush, but not much more.

Each of them is right—from their perspectives. The Guardian Way does call back to the past, it is shrouded in legend, and it can better the individual by helping to transcend comfort zones. Imprinted in our DNA, the Guardian archetype is part of our biological programming. Every time we reach out beyond ourselves to help another, we are the Guardian. Whenever we feel the urge to take a risk and show our courage, it is the Guardian in us coming alive. When fear prickles our blood, it is our Guardian voice calling us to action.

Despite what I consider to be an obvious argument for the intrinsic value of the Guardian Way, some people still come back with their original questions about where and how it applies and how it can help them. To me, the Guardian motto, *only actions speak,* suggests that the philosophy, science, and history behind the Guardian Way are far less important than the actual practice. The greater concern of mine is what happens when the practice comes to a halt. To me, an inactive Guardian is a pitiful couch potato. There is so much energy brewing in the heart of a Guardian that to not let it out is to go against Nature. If I were inactive, I couldn't live with myself. In fact, I would question whether I was living at all.

Fortunately, I feel alive every day because I find innumerable ways to serve others while still conducting my daily affairs. It takes no great effort, and I don't need to consciously stay in a Guardian mindset. It has become a way of life; I intuitively recognize opportunities and automatically step into service.

In doing so, I keep honing my skills and maturing as a Guardian. This strengthening is inevitable, and it takes little or no extra effort because after all, training is life and life is training.

The following are some ways that the Guardian in me is called into service in my everyday activities. I share them in hopes that they will help you see the various ways that we can seamlessly integrate the Guardian mindset into our daily lives.

- When traveling by air, I take an emergency exit seat whenever possible, so that I can be responsible for it.
- I wait until everyone else has exited a plane, bus, car, train, boat, or elevator before I exit.
- When I'm with others and there are parcels to carry, I take the heaviest or most awkward ones.
- I hold doors for people less able than me (which is not out of politeness or because of gender bias).
- I take the least comfortable seat.
- I take perimeter positions in groups, jump to service when needed, and stay attuned to the surroundings.
- I eat the scraps and pan scrapings.
- I create pedestals for others to show their talents and serve their people.

- I provide training opportunities for my people who are Guardians.

- Wherever I go, I pick up litter that disfigures the Mother's countenance. I reserve my left pants pocket for whatever fits in it.

- When I determine that a panhandler is likely going to buy alcohol, I recognize that it's not my place to judge another's life, so I often give him money and wish him a good time.

Of course, your life is different than mine. We have different habits, relationships, and responsibilities. Still, we have a remarkable amount in common. When we embrace the spirit of the Guardian Way, opportunities to serve jump out at us at every turn. In fact, it comes to the point where serving others no longer feels like an opportunity—or even like serving. It just becomes the normal, everyday thing to do.

PART II

THE MINDSET

The man of wood sings,

the woman of stone

gets up and dances.

This cannot be done

by passion or learning,

it cannot be done

by reasoning.

— Tung-shan Liang-chieh, medieval Chinese Zen teacher[1]

CHAPTER 7

THE DRIVING FORCE

We all want to be passionate about something. It's a great motivator, and we admire others who are enthusiastic about what they do. However, a father isn't always excited about taking care of his sick child in the middle of the night. Still, it has to be done. The last thing an exhausted and bone-chilled backcountry skier wants to do is dig through the snow for firewood to warm her hypothermic companion. Still, it has to be done.

Passion is not what usually pulls survivors through situations where others perish. Survivors draw from a deeper, more consistent and reliable reservoir, which I call *circle consciousness*. That reservoir gets filled by leading a life based on the premise that *giving is receiving*. If you've ever felt the warm glow of giving something to somebody who deeply appreciated it, you intrinsically understand the meaning of *giving is receiving*.

When we give, we nurture relationship—both with our inner selves and with others. These relationships are what sustain us in both good times and bad. When we give first to others, we create trust and encourage openness. When others have a food or supply surplus, or when I am in need, the chances are good that they will take care of me. In times of crisis, we naturally draw upon this reservoir of benevolence and care that we have stored up within ourselves.

We take care of ourselves in the same way. In doing so we maintain perspective on our state of being, along with considering the overall cause and effect of our actions.

The Guardian Is Steadfast

There is a big difference between *steadfastness* and *stubbornness*, which has everything to do with the way we involve ourselves in a given situation. Steadfastness implies persistence, commitment, and focus. However, it can quickly become stubbornness if we stick to something against all odds, and in the process lose perspective. When we refuse to let go, we imperil ourselves—and possibly the Mission. We are no longer steadfast, but stubborn. We are no longer centered in our Heart-of-Hearts, no longer coming from a place of empathy. Our ego and emotions have taken over and we have become passionate. Empathy is considerate; passion is blind.

The term *passionate Guardian* is an oxymoron. Someone who becomes passionate is no longer a Guardian. He may be a Warrior, he may be a soldier for a cause, he may be a mercenary, he may be a martyr—but he is not a Guardian.

The reason—and the core reason we need to be dispassionate on Missions—is because the brain has *coherence.* When one part of our brain dominates, other parts become less active. When our amygdala (the region of the brain that controls fear and longing) is overactive with anxiety and hyper-vigilance, our frontal lobe (which calmly evaluates and plans) is underactive. Hence the state of mind we have all experienced when we are anxious and on guard and at the same time not able to perform as well as usual.

Where Willfulness Lurks

In order to function dispassionately, the Guardian needs to remain as free-flowing as water in a stream: ready to twist with the bends, ride the riffles, and split to go around rocks. Any willfulness on the part of the Guardian interferes with the continuous and steady nature of the stream. Herein lies a dilemma for the Guardian-in-training, as many popular consciousness-raising exercises he could use are willful. Meditation, yoga, and fasting are examples. With training, what is important is not so much what we do, but how we do it. Even though willful exercises provide us with some benefits, the willful imprint on our *limbic process*, which is our subconscious mind and control center, remains. A fast comes and goes, a yoga posture can be learned and forgotten, yet the willfulness we used in their practice does not fade. The more we train ourselves to act willfully, the less likely we are to act intuitively in times of crisis or on a Mission. Actions based on conscious thought (i.e., willful actions) are self-limiting, as they are dependent on learned behaviors and they often enlist courage and adrenaline as helpers. Although on the surface they seem to help, they further limit our adaptability and instinctual capabilities.

The Guardian functions best when she is dispassionate, and willfulness is a characteristic of passion. Here is yet another reason that for the Guardian, *training is life*. There is no need to willfully set aside training time or choose training modalities, as every thought and action is training. Although training exercises are helpful, it's the effortless daily Guardian mindset that really shapes and strengthens the Trainee.

It Takes Courage?

Have courage is a well-used line, usually intended to bolster someone who is faltering. Most of us hold the image of the Guardian as a courageous upholder of her people's well-being, always at the ready to boldly step forward and serve. All of that is true—except for the courageous and bold part. For the Guardian, courage can be just as crippling as fear. "How can that be?" I'm sure some of you are asking. "Isn't courage the opposite of fear?"

To see courage as such is only a trick of the mind, which creates the courage-fear dichotomy to motivate us. The reason we can switch so easily between the two is that they are really the same core emotion, which is *fear*. The only distinguishing characteristic between the two is that courage is active (it motivates) and fear is passive (it cripples).

When we respond to fear with courage, we never get to know our fear. Instead, we create an endless stimulus-response loop, which results in the habit of continually addressing fear with courage. Disguising fear with courage keeps us disconnected from the core reason we are compelled to mask our fear with courage in the first place. Instead of being engaged in conscious responses to situations, we become adrenaline-stoked aggressive-defensive weapons. It's all we are capable of, as our natural abilities to center ourselves and engage in constructive and creative conflict-resolution processes have been impaired.

Whether we call it courage or fear, when the Guardian is infused with either she is running on something other than *Mission Consciousness*. She has her own agenda, which makes her prone to heroics and functioning independently of the pack. In order for the Guardian to be effective, she needs to be a nonentity. Courage is for soldiers and heroes, and the medals of honor go to them. The Guardian has no name or face; she is as anonymous and unfeeling as a shadow. She sees what the hero never will, and she is able to go places and do things that the Soldier-Warrior could never imagine, much less execute. The Guardian's actions are the antithesis of courageous: They are cold, calculated, and disconnected.

For the Guardian, there is no reason for performing her actions other than to benefit the Mission itself. Just as the heart beats and the lungs breathe, the Guardian carries out her part of the Mission. There is no need for courage. In training, the Guardian works to dwell in the reality beyond courage and fear. Whenever she gets captured by either, she knows to withdraw from the Training—and especially from a Mission—as she has become a liability. No matter what her courage might help her achieve, it is now she who is functioning, not an organ that has completely given itself to the organism. Any emotional charge not only blinds and cripples the

Guardian, but also reduces the likelihood of Mission success. Let's leave courage to the Rambos and martyrs, and instead serve our people by acting intelligently and consciously to help assure the success of our Missions.

What Motivates the Guardian

We have two main motivations: fear and longing. Whether it is personal fulfillment, family matters, or service to others, we can trace our reason for engagement to either fear or longing. This may seem to be an oversimplified explanation of the forces that motivate us. However, before you judge:

1. Choose a couple of your own significant involvements that you don't think are motivated by fear or longing.
2. Deeply examine why you have engaged in them.
3. If you initially come up with nothing, look at whether there might be another fear or longing-based situation that prevents you from seeing deeper.

What, then, motivates the Guardian?

For a moment, set aside the assumption that we need motivation to function. The Guardian trains to approach a Mission like breathing—it's just something she does, with no thought about success or failure or what it might bring to her or others. Service is not even a motivating factor. When the Guardian says that *the Mission is life, and life is the Mission*, it is the same as saying that *breathing is life and life is breathing*. There cannot be anything more than that, as it would only interfere with the execution of a Mission, in the same way that getting consciously engaged in our breathing process would only interfere with its perfect, natural execution.

How to Maintain Dispassionate Perspective

In order to be ever-aware, the Guardian needs to be ever-observant. To allow for this, she must do two things:

▪ Remain dispassionate.

▪ Engage in *soft looking and hearing*.

Maintaining sensory perception without focusing on any particular sight or sound is the way of soft looking and hearing. *Hard looking* is focused sight, and *hard hearing* is focused listening. When we become emotionally engaged in something, or when we are overly determined or passionate, we automatically switch to hard looking and hearing. This is a fight-flight survival response that helps us focus on the immediacy of the moment.

However, in situations that do not call for a survival response, hard looking and hearing cripples. For the Guardian to be both effective and adaptive to the unexpected, she must remain dispassionate. Dispassion encourages *soft looking and hearing*, which is so much our natural predisposition that we need to consciously override it when we want to focus on something specific.

Many of us end up regularly overriding our soft sensory approach because we live in a society that constantly bombards us with stimuli, much of which is technologically based and commands short bursts of attention. This has caused a permanent shift toward *hard sensory perception*.

To retrain yourself to use soft sensory perception

Practice soft sensory perception by letting fear-based feelings flow through you, as they are what keeps you locked in hard sensory perception mode. Because we are feeling beings, there is no effective way to deny or suppress those fear-based feelings—they inevitably come back. The reason is that all feelings have their reasons, so we continually acknowledge and process them on a subconscious level. The trick is to acknowledge them without feeding them.

The problem arises when the conscious mind gets involved in the process. A feeling's lifespan is around 90 seconds, which gives us enough time to fully experience it, process it, and respond if necessary. The conscious mind, however, can dwell on the feeling, which gives us another 90 seconds with it, and so on. The loop continues as long as the conscious mind stays engaged.

If the feeling does not immediately serve us, it is best to let it go and trust in our subconscious process, which is far more aware and capable than our conscious process. Unbeknownst to us on a conscious level, our subconscious mind runs the show. It takes care of 95 to 99 percent of our decision making, along with governing our social and emotional lives and storing the long-term memories from which we continually draw.[2]

Now for the Ego

In effect, you who are training in soft looking and listening are re-learning to trust in your natural abilities. The impediment to trust is none other than your ego, which has faith only in what it has at its immediate disposal and can consciously control— and that is the rational mind. In order to get you to relinquish control to the dynamic duo (the ego and the rational mind), the ego will manipulate you with your own feelings. The ego has no scruples; it is designed to be amoral and deadly effective.

To stay in the driver's seat, the ego manipulates you by getting you caught up in the dog-chasing-her-tail feeling loop that we just discussed. The ego can then control you by controlling your feelings.

When you find yourself caught up in the loop, here is a three-step method to escape it:

1. **Relax,** to reduce stress and get out of fight-flight mode.
2. **Breathe,** to re-center yourself and regain perspective.
3. **Reconnect** with your Heart-of-Hearts, to again hear your inner guidance.

Use any relaxation, conscious breathing, and deep listening techniques that work for you. They all bring about the same result: allowing you to yield to the subconscious mind and effortlessly engage with your surroundings and the beings who inhabit it, which is the foundation of the Guardian Way.

Chapter 7 Citations

1   Tung-shan Liang-chieh, "Song of Precious Mirror Samadhi," Sacred Texts, https://www.sacred-texts.com/bud/zen/hz/hz.htm (accessed October 11, 2019).

2   Daniel Goleman, "New View of Mind Gives Unconscious Expanded Role," The New York Times, February 7, 1984.

CHAPTER 8

STRENGTH FROM GOING WITH THE RIVER

We have learned that the Guardian's approach needs to be objective and dispassionate, so that we can be fully present and adaptable. We then have unfettered access to our energy and intuitive abilities. The concept of conflict runs contrary to this approach, as it sets us up in opposition to an external force. The antagonistic energy thus created triggers our fight-flight mechanism. We instinctively respond by positioning ourselves to either defend or attack. Adrenaline and cortisone wash through our system, empowering us to our maximum capacity.

However, the fight-flight response also narrows our focus, limits our perspective, and eventually depletes us of physical and emotional energy. Notice how when you are tense or angry, you see nothing but what is right in front of you, and your entire being is consumed by what has triggered your condition. That is adrenaline at work. Then notice how drained you feel after a confrontation. That is what adrenaline leaves you with after finishing its job.

Needless to say, our fight-flight response runs contrary to our ability to be objective and dispassionate in order to be present and adaptable when we are in service. This chapter takes us deep into the bowels of conflict, so that we can see it for the illusion it is. We will then learn how to work *with*, rather than against, the forces that would otherwise morph into conflict.

For the sake of illustration, I am going to create a simple, dichotomous comparison between Guardian and Warrior approaches. In actual practice, there are similarities along with differences, and there is no definitive line between the two.

Conflict—The Guardian Way

In the classic Warrior mentality, there are enemies. Soldiers are brainwashed into the enemy mentality by persistent calls to dehumanize and hate a people who are classed as their opponents. Sports teams and businesses adopt an enemy mentality in order to outperform a competitor. It has gone to such an extreme that we wage wars on poverty and fight for peace—which has to be the ultimate oxymoron.

The approach might work for some people, but not for the Guardian. A game and a fight are over quickly, but not so with a Mission. For the Guardian, the Mission is life and life is the Mission. There is no opponent or game time to supercharge him. There is not even a specific training or field exercise time, as life is the training, and the training is the Guardian's life. He is ever ready, as a Mission could be called at any time. In fact, he could be in some phase of performing a Mission and not even be aware of it. This approach keeps the Guardian dispassionate, fully present, and engaged, with little hormonal overcharge to pump him up and burn him out. This is the secret behind the Guardian's ability to perform what sometimes seem to be superhuman feats, such as pulling off complex Missions in the face of tremendous odds and performing for an entire day or more without food or rest.

At any time on a Mission, a well-functioning Guardian could be examined and you would not find the choppy breathing, tensed muscles, or narrowly focused eyes of someone fueled by adrenaline. If the Mission were called off that moment, he could sit down and have a normal conversation with you without having to first cool down and re-center himself.

Martial Arts and the Guardian

I'm often asked how martial arts fit into the Guardian Way. Most people mean contemporary martial arts, which differ in some fundamental ways from martial arts as they were traditionally practiced. We see the differences in today's training and competitions, which carry hallmarks of the Warrior approach we just discussed. The modern martial arts practitioner has set times of practice, scheduled bouts, and a clearly defined enemy. Her Training focuses on developing the strength and dexterity to defeat her opponent.

An example of the traditional roots of martial arts can be found in Ninjitsu, a surviving classical Japanese practice based on stealth, invisibility, and cunning. The Ninja moves as a shadow and is seldom, if ever, seen. Her ways are shrouded in mystery and her feats are legendary. Yet, as is distinctive of the Guardian Way, her methods have little or nothing to do with courage, strength, or overpowering anyone.

One way to tell the difference between how a Warrior and a Guardian work with conflict is that the Guardian response is often unpredictable and seemingly spontaneous, while the Warrior response is typically preplanned, as it is with scheduled martial arts sessions.

Go with the Flow Training

If there is any secret to the seamless functioning of a Guardian, no matter what is thrown at her, it is *aligning with the energies at play*. It doesn't matter if those energies are complementary or combative. However, there are some clear benefits to having more alignment than resistance on Missions, as well as in our daily lives.

Why Resistance Hurts

- It takes energy.
- It diminishes awareness to surroundings.

- It consumes valuable time.
- It distracts from the Mission.
- It makes us conspicuous, which ups the odds for interference and Mission failure.

Why Alignment Helps

- It contributes energy.
- It reduces stress and distraction.
- It heightens silence and invisibility.
- It opens options for adapting and adjusting.
- It increases the odds for Mission success.

The problem is that our culture conditions us for combativeness rather than alignment. Here is a story that shows how our conditioning consumes and narrows us and how much easier it would be to fulfill the Mission if we were in *alignment consciousness*:

Three Beggars who were traveling together came upon a coin lying in the road.

"I want to buy something to eat with it," stated the first Beggar.

"I want several things to eat," asserted the second.

"That cannot be!" shouted the third. "I want something to drink!"

While they stood there arguing, an Elder came along and offered to help them come to a resolution.

"Yes!" they all exclaimed. "Please choose which of us shall have his desire fulfilled."

"If you will give me your coin," suggested the Elder, "I will do just that."

Just ahead was a roadside produce stand. The Elder bought a basket of melons and brought it back to the Beggars.

"Aha! I now have something to eat!" rejoiced the first Beggar as he reached for a melon.

"That is not correct," stated the second, "for here I have a *few* things to eat."

"You are both wrong," accused the third, "for this is clearly something to satisfy my thirst."

Alignment Consciousness Training

Fortunately, it is easy to train for alignment consciousness. One thing that we use so much that we take it for granted—our thumb—serves as a tool to incorporate alignment-consciousness training into our everyday lives.

One popular theory in human evolution is that our opposable thumbs gave our hominid ancestors the capacity to begin evolving intellectual abilities that set us apart from other animals. Yet, not all has come up roses with what our opposable thumbs have wrought. The ability to make and wield tools has given us bulldozers, oil wells, and thermonuclear bombs, which have wreaked havoc upon our Mother Planet and our Balance-centered way of life.

Let's use the opposable thumb as a metaphor for our ability to work in opposition to the natural flow of things. The following exercises eliminate the thumb, which forces us to find ways to go with the flow. In doing so, we become sensitized to accomplishing things without forcing them; that is, without opposing the energies that be. These energies are there to help us, yet we have to first recognize them, then learn how to utilize them. To accomplish that, here are three effective exercises:

1. No-Thumb Paddling

A canoe is designed to slip effortlessly through the water, and so is a paddle. The only reason the paddle doesn't slice seamlessly in and out of the water is that we think we have to force it in order to propel the canoe. This is a myth based on our tool culture, which instructs us to impose our will over our environment, to alter it so it will better suit our needs.

However, there is no need to alter a water environment for a canoe to traverse it effectively, and there is no need to grip a paddle like a typical tool in order to transfer our energy into forward motion. When we become the paddle and our canoe becomes an extension of our skin, we can work together smoothly and effortlessly, as if we are walking a woodland trail. Here's how it's done:

a) **Lay the paddle in your hands** as though you are going to use it, but without wrapping your thumbs around the handle.

b) **Pull the paddle through the water,** letting the water and the rhythm of the stroke keep the paddle stable.

c) **Lift the paddle from the water,** letting the weight of the paddle, rather than your thumbs, keep it connected to you.

d) **Repeat the motion** in one graceful, sinuous flow. The more rhythmic and the less jerky your movements, the less you will be compelled to resort to using your thumbs for control. Instead, you will learn to rely on presence, conscious engagement, and reading the natural forces at play, rather than imposing force to counter and manipulate what already exists.

It is opposing force that creates disturbance. When our energy and flow complements what already exists, we exert minimal effort and move silently and invisibly.

For a video demonstration, google *Teaching Drum Outdoor School–YouTube*, then click on *Solo Canoeing Workshop.*

2. No-Thumb Tool Use

I just finished raking the leaves in my mother's lawn, without the use of my thumbs. I could have done it

faster by gripping the rake in typical fashion and mus-
cling my way through the task, but it would have taken
more energy and created more disturbance. Just as
important, I would have been less consciously engaged
in the process. I found a rhythm with the rake that was
much like paddling; the tool became an extension of
my arms, and the leaves came together as though they
were waves rolling up on a beach.

True to the precept that *Life is training and training
is life*, I naturally raked with no thumbs because it is the
way I paddle and use some other tools, such as shovels.
It came easily, as I was accustomed to the go-with-the-
flow approach. On a Mission, I will naturally use the same
approach, which will increase the chances of success.

3. No-Thumb Writing

I often take notes during the day, whether it is on my
calendar, in my notebook, or on a Post-It. Though it felt
awkward at first, I can now let the pencil lie comfortably
between my index and middle finger while it flows along
with the movements of my hand and my thoughts.

Since I don't rely on force for writing, my ideas flow
more freely than before, which has helped me become
a more clear and expressive writer. Like the paddle and
the rake, the pencil has become more of an extension of
myself than a tool that I force to do my bidding.

I have given three examples of what can be done by not
doing. Use them as metaphors for moving as effortlessly and
silently as a shadow by utilizing already existing energies rather
than your own. There are many activities in our daily lives for
which the thumb is unnecessary. Whenever you discover one of
them, you can turn it into an unexpected training exercise. Keep
track of the opportunities you find and compare notes with your
fellow Trainees.

Deconstructing the Enemy Concept

Enemies are a construct of the mind. We create them by thinking them into existence. Thinking in itself is not the problem; we couldn't survive for more than an instant without it. Issues arise when we begin formulating thoughts from our thinking. We then separate and categorize our thoughts, creating dichotomies. In doing so, we train ourselves to practice *divided thinking*, rather than *integrative thinking*, or what my Elders call the *Circle Way of thinking.*

Imagine the act of thinking to be a forest comprised of Trees, Birds, Monkeys, Elephants, and the Clouds overhead. When we distinguish these life forms from each other and treat them separately, we create dichotomies: useful/not useful, threatening/not threatening, beautiful/ugly. These dichotomies encourage us to create distinct appraisals and value judgments about each of these life-forms rather than seeing them all as interconnected and important in their own right.

The reason we often think like this is out of fear or yearning: Either we want something from the Forest or we want to protect ourselves from something in the Forest—a clear dichotomy. In the same way, we create enemies, which are purely constructs of the mind.

The enemy concept gets in the way of the functioning of the dispassionate Guardian because it triggers our fight-flight response. No more can we remain dispassionate and maintain perspective. We have converted from *soft looking (perspective)* to *hard looking (focus),* and in doing so we have greatly decreased the inner and outer resources available to us. *Whenever the enemy mindset surfaces, the Guardian must either re-center herself in dispassion or disengage from the Mission. She has become a peril to both herself and the Mission, and she cannot take the risk of proceeding under those circumstances.* If the Guardian is not aware of her state and someone else in the Mission is, it is the responsibility of that individual to call it out and not proceed with the Mission until the Guardian in enemy consciousness disengages. If one organ is dysfunctional, the entire organism is compromised. Not only will the pack falter, but the Mission will be jeopardized as well. Therefore, it is the responsibility of any pack member aware of another who has slipped into enemy consciousness to act quickly. When dispassion is reinstated throughout the entire organism, Pack Consciousness can once again be realized.

CHAPTER 9

TRANSPARENCY IN SERVICE

There is a Zen saying that when we look for something to stand on, a voice is telling us, "Stand on nothing." This has a special meaning for the Guardian, who strives to move as discreetly as a shadow and to seamlessly blend with her environment.

It all starts with the Training. This is an ad we run for the Guardian Way Training Program:

WANTED

A few daring souls willing to leave all you know behind:
your beliefs, your friends, your comforts
Who are willing to risk everything
— even your own identity —
to serve your people and your Mother Earth
For you, the Guardian Way awaits

Notice that the first thing listed to leave behind is beliefs. Astonishingly resilient, they reflect the norms and expectations of our culture, and they are the primary means of perpetuating cultural priorities. Beliefs create identities and feed the ego. They are so all-pervasive that when many of us hear the word *Truth* or *viewpoint*, we think *belief*.

The Guardian needs a more immediate Truth than anything she could glean from a belief. She needs to function from what she is thinking and feeling *right here and now*. This moment dictates her next move and the move after that. Although beliefs tend to have only a minimal influence on the moment at hand, because they encompass so many moments in the past, they can be a major obstacle in *envisioning* and planning a Mission. They can be particularly problematic when it is necessary to redesign a Mission that is not going according to script.

From Zen and healing perspectives, here are some of the many ways beliefs run contrary to Guardian Consciousness:

- They keep us from seeing beyond what we think we know, which makes us resistant to new ideas and possibilities.
- Holding onto them can create misery.
- They have inherent contradictions.
- They determine how we conduct ourselves.
- We feel compelled to defend them, which can lead to conflict.
- We use them as excuses.
- They burden us with thoughts irrelevant to the now, which distracts us from the moment.
- When they change, they disrupt our ability to envision our future.
- They cause us to value conceptual over pragmatic thinking.
- We latch onto other people's beliefs to compensate for what we lack.
- They create vested interests and blind spots, which result in tunnel thinking.
- They filter and put a spin on everything we see.
- We function on conviction rather than knowledge, which casts doubt on what we do.
- They trigger inappropriate emotional responses.
- The stronger we hold on to them, the truer their opposites appear.

- They rob us of presence, so we merely go through the motions of living.
- They can give us false confidence.
- When they change, we question prior decisions based upon earlier beliefs.

To sum it all up, beliefs mask or distort the voice of the Heart-of-Hearts, which is our seat of centeredness. It's where our emotions, intuition, ancestral memories, ego, and mind sit together in council to guide us. The Heart-of-Hearts is like a reflective pool, which neither takes nor reaches out for anything. Beliefs would have us do both.

How to Train around Beliefs

The first step is never to think, "I don't have beliefs." There is a belief attached to everything we see, do, and say. This is necessary in order to help us make sense of our surroundings and relationships. To suddenly drop our personal beliefs is impossible.

Yet there is one thing we Trainees must do in order to develop as Guardians: We must break our *attachment* to our beliefs. Although beliefs help us function, attachment to them leads us away from Guardian Consciousness. A Guardian tosses a belief aside as quickly and easily as a wrong-size wrench. Guardian Training involves breaking our attachment to our beliefs, old and new. This frees us to clearly see what our beliefs had masked.

When I'm asked how we can tell when we are hung up on beliefs, I have one simple answer: It creates tension. I learned this from living with a pack of Wolves. When they were relaxed and flowing with the now, there were times when I felt agitated. I came to realize that it was because I was holding onto a belief of how things should be. My agitation did not allow me to accept what was and immerse myself in it, which put me out of sync with the pack.

It also put me out of sync with myself, because I was nothing without my pack. I had no identity, I could not function, and I had no sense of purpose. In the end, I could not survive without them. Yet what affected me most in the moment was that I could not feel the camaraderie and enjoy their presence.

The greatest benefit of releasing our attachment to beliefs is that we become more effective as individuals *and* in a group. I cannot stress how important this is, since beliefs to which we remain attached create a veil for the fearful Trainee to hide behind. We can't seriously begin training until we humble ourselves by giving up the security of our cherished beliefs.

To get out from under the controlling nature of beliefs:

1. **Utilize Wisdom.** The Zen Masters say that the more aware we are of the poison of attachment, the more we will be inspired to abandon our marriage to old beliefs.

2. **Look Back.** Reflection shows us that the beliefs that guide us are all false, because over time they rewrite our history and change what we think we know. We see that they shackle us.

3. **Become Functional.** When we override our egos and force ourselves to function as pack members, we can't help but see that beliefs are the antithesis of effectiveness. When we realize this, the beliefs cease to have meaning.

"Don't we need beliefs to keep us from being amoral?" I've been asked more than once.

"Not Guardians," I reply. "They have a different reason for being and a unique sense of purpose, which is Missions. To serve their people is their soul and to perfect their Mission skills is their lifeblood."

For anyone who still has trouble accepting the premise that attachment to beliefs is unwise, I suggest meditating on this ancient Zen aphorism:

> *The only beliefs worth holding are*
> *the ones known by three-year-olds.*

How Do We Tell If We are Attached to Beliefs?

People ask me this question often enough—and it is important enough—that I want to give it a thorough answer. I'll start by stating that if I am not "a walkin' contradiction, partly Truth and partly fiction," as singer Kris Kristofferson says, I am attached to beliefs.

I do sometimes seem to be full of contradictions. Some people wonder why they can ask me the same question twice and get two different answers—without me feeling the need to recant anything or justify myself. Others don't see how I can treat one person one way and another person another way.

So what does "partly Truth and partly fiction" mean? For this discussion, I would say that Truth is what I believe in, and fiction is what I do not believe in. My rational mind works to keep me aligned to my Truth, which becomes my belief system.

If I were not a walking contradiction, I would be stuck in my rational mind, continually trying to be true to my beliefs. Or if I were caught up in a victimization-enabling paradigm, I might try to hold onto someone else's belief of who or how I should be.

Many people consider it a gift to be true to a belief, which amounts to being stuck in our rational minds. This is easy to do within a culture that places a high value on logic, deductive reasoning, and associative thinking. We deeply regard consistency; we look up to those who stick to their beliefs. We mistrust contradiction, and we interpret those who change their beliefs to be flaky or fickle. Is it any surprise then, that Guardians in believer societies are often seen as walking contradictions, mistrusted, marginalized, and even exiled?

Attempting to function in a believer society can come at a cost to Guardians—a great cost. If we succumb to the pressure to live by our culture's Truths and beliefs, we must devote our rational processes to not contradicting those Truths and beliefs.

Our problem is that the rational mind is an enslaved mind. Its operating system is bound to what can be intellectually grasped, quantified, and replicated. It is fixed to consistency, which means *no contradictions*. At the same time, let's remember that everything we see, do, and say is based upon beliefs. What this boils down to is that when we function from the rational mind, we are enslaved to beliefs—both ours and others'. This moves us further and further from the voice of our Heart-of-Hearts.

The Guardian Way demands that we be walking contradictions, ever alert to the changes around us and changing with them. We re-envision and readjust as these changes occur, exploring the fiction beyond Truth. When we are fixed to our personal and cultural beliefs, we are enacting the antithesis of the Guardian Way.

Belief Relief

Our liberation comes from realizing that yielding to the rational mind is yet another belief that we allow to influence us. If we could see beyond our ego (the rational mind's front man) and be brutally honest with ourselves, we would see that we are enslaved not by our minds per se, but by a belief system. Enslavement is the only way the rational mind can be brought to accept the self-imposed limitations that beliefs bring.

This is a functioning mode that goes against our intrinsic Nature. In other words, a rational mind hobbled by personal and cultural beliefs makes sense only because we believe it makes sense.

Here are some indications that we are caught up in beliefs that limit our ability to be flexible and contradictory, and therefore transparent in our service to others:

- We are prone to arguing.
- We have trouble doing anything in a way other than "my way."

- We criticize and label.

- We find it difficult to listen to a viewpoint other than our own.

- We struggle to accept another person's reality that differs from ours.

- We would judge someone who gave a begging drunk some money and told him to go and have a good time.

- We would rather suffer or terminate a relationship than change our ways in order to create a healthier relationship.

- We would fight and die for a belief.

Don't feel bad if you can relate to most of these points—at least, don't feel any worse than I do. I'd be more surprised if anyone (myself included) didn't recognize these traits in him or herself from time to time. Realizing where we are in the belief-attachment process allows us to continue to work on separating from our beliefs, so that we can be a solid asset to our Mission pack.

CHAPTER 10

WHAT BREEDS FAILURE

Accidents happen, right? Let's, for a moment, adopt an inquisitive mind and imagine that there are no such things as accidents. And for good measure, let's throw in background noise, wasted time, daydreams, happenstance, or even trash. Let's further imagine that to write anything off as such would be a denial of the reason for our intelligence, which is to make sense of seemingly random and unrelated occurrences.

Bad luck and fate, then, would merely reflect our inability to consciously process what is going on in our lives. Instead, we first victimize ourselves, then we externalize the situations by blaming others, which creates the "bad things happen to me" mindset.

If one were to ask a Native about mistakes, failures, or accidents, she would likely reply that they do not exist. Hawaiian Elder Kaili'ohe Kame'ekua, who lived in the 1800s, put it this way: "We were taught from the time we could understand that there are no accidents. All things happen for a reason. We may not know what the reason is at the moment. Be happy even for misfortune, for with it comes some wisdom that we could not have had otherwise."[1] One of my favorite bits of folk wisdom is the German saying *Ein guter Stolperer fällt nicht*, which means "A good stumbler falleth not."[2]

Imagine if those of us who felt victimized by accidents, failures, and mistakes empowered ourselves by embracing them as eye-openers, teachers, and opportunities. I've seen this simple change in perspective transform people's lives. Yes, this attitude adjustment is monumental—even revolutionary—yet when we accomplish it, what we have really done is returned to the outlook we were born with.

Our Children Can Help Us Remember

When we were kids, we intrinsically knew the Zen saying that failure teaches success. Perhaps the greatest gift our children could bestow upon us is helping us relearn this core training precept through their example.

My mate Lety sums up this approach to training with a favorite proverb of hers: *Failure is not an option—it is a privilege reserved only for those who try.* Anthropologist Margaret Mead shares a unique twist on our beliefs around failure from the Iatmul people of New Guinea: "We laugh at a failure—at a slip of the tongue, at someone who stumbles clumsily where grace is required. The Iatmul, on the other hand, laugh uproariously when a child or a foreigner gets something right."[3] Noted Vermont lawyer and diplomat Edward John Phelps cut to the quick when he said, "The man who makes no mistakes does not usually make anything."

For those who still insist on being victimized by life—and in turn victimize their children—I would like to offer this sage morsel: he who thinks he was never a fool is now a fool. When my son Wabineshi was young, we would make a game of humbling ourselves with statements like, "How silly of me; if I didn't learn something from that, I deserve it twice as bad next time." If the simplest thing we can do to grow in wisdom is to admit we're fools, we'd be fools not to.

Revel in Failure

In our Training, the word *failure* is never mentioned. When something doesn't work, it's cause to celebrate, as it shows a weak point that needs attention. Entirely successful trainings, especially when they occur time after time, are a waste of time and energy. They do two things:

- They create a false sense of security.
- They do not train for the worst-case scenarios that can occur on a Mission.

It's far better that "mistakes" come up in training than on a Mission, so that they can be worked out and the lessons can be learned. In this way, the pack grows more adaptable and resilient. Each pack member learns to take more personal responsibility for her actions.

Training is designed to be tough in order to push the pack to its edge and create failures. The fewer the failures, the tougher the Training has to get in order to create more failures. The empowered Guardian loves failure-based training and thrives on it.

Keep Trying?

"I'll keep trying," means "I'll keep doing the same thing over and over, hoping it will eventually work." First of all, there is no room for *trying* in the Guardian Way. Missions are approached with a do-or-die attitude—and sometimes do or die is literally the case. "Let's give it a go and see what happens," is the antithesis of the Guardian Way. Guardians *do* because the livelihood of the pack and the welfare of our people depend on it. *Try* is not in our vocabulary.

Secondly, when we try, we are not fully engaged. We have one foot in and one foot out, to cover ourselves in case we fail. Such an approach considerably increases the odds that the Mission will fail, as we are neither fully present nor committed. Does it make sense to engage in something that we have already undermined? Is this the way we want to serve our people?

Rather than the mindset "We'll try it," imagine what the "We'll do it!" mindset would do to encourage Pack Consciousness and contribute to Mission success.

The Matter of Choice

A confused mind is a Guardian's bane. As soon as I think I have to make a choice—or even that I have a choice I could make—I switch from clarity to confusion:

- I am not able to act spontaneously.
- I am not able to clearly read sensory input.
- I lose centeredness and focus.
- I compromise my ability to be a fully present and functioning pack member.

The issue is not whether or not I have choices; dualistic perspective (which creates choices) is merely a trick of the rational mind to simplify reality. It's not that there are no choices in the natural realm—*there is always and only one choice: survival.* When I have to act, there is no option to put everything on hold and consider another option, or even to recognize that there are options. It's either do or die.

Of course, in most cases it's not literally do or die. However, organisms evolved processing and responsive capacities for worst-case scenarios, as these capacities were the determining factors for whether or not the organism survived to pass on successful adaptive traits. So even though a situation may not literally be do or die, we still handle it with our do-or-die circuitry. In this sense, to entertain the notion of choices is to dance with death. On the way there, I become enslaved by my rational mind, which keeps me anxious and disconnected. Rather than living in the now, I merely exist. In the world of choices, I question whether true joy is possible. Every decision carries doubt with it, and every action drags the weight of the other action it could have been.

Choice During Missions

In planning a Mission, two goals are paramount: *maximize success* and *minimize risk.* It's the same on the Hunt, where the two goals are to *get the animal* and *live on to get another*. If we don't succeed the first time, our growling bellies and screaming children will make sure we do the next time.

When I keep these two goals in mind during each step of the planning, there is always only one choice immediately before me: to be well-practiced and have a solid plan. That's survival. Otherwise, I am relying on trial and error, and my people will starve.

However, this doesn't mean that every step of the Mission is set in stone. Inflexibility in Missions is amateurish and carries a high risk. On a mature Guardian Mission, there is constant fine-tuning, which is why continual and effective communication is important. Effective communication is clear communication, which means concise, direct, and without the uncertainty that leads to shaky choices. (We'll get into communication in depth in Part IV.)

The Essential Value of Trust

Guardians need the trust of their people and vice versa. Without the mutual trust of pack members, a Mission is no more than a game of chance. The Guardian pack is built on trust—so much so that when any mistrust arises, it is immediately addressed and eliminated. There are no exceptions.

How often have you heard or spoken these lines?

– "I trusted you! How could you do that to me?"
– "You let me down."
– "I didn't think you were that kind of person."
– Or on the enabling side: "I'm so sorry, I didn't mean to hurt you."

I've used similar lines, and I remember how I felt at the time. I was angry and hurt. Along with that, I grew resentful and judgmental. In the heat of the moment, I told myself I wasn't going to trust anymore. The next time, I would be wiser and more cautious. I would keep my eyes open and not be so gullible. They were all reactive responses spoken by my ego, who wanted to protect me.

Yet there was an element of Truth to my ego's voice that would have served me well to hear. There is a saying that *Love is blind*, but that is not entirely accurate. The saying should be *Trust is blind*. Only fools trust, which all of us know who have been made fools of by trusting.

The reason is that trust as we define and practice it is a projection. If I say to my five-year-old child, "I trusted you; why did you run out in the street?" I have projected an expectation upon her that she was incapable of fulfilling. Expectations are not trust; they are dysfunctional behaviors. *Trust is knowing and respecting*. When I know and respect others for who and how they are, I meet them where they are rather than creating expectations by projecting my ego-based needs or woundedness on them.

The quotes that open this section on trust all say the same thing I said to my child in the street: I projected an expectation on you, and you did not meet it. Trust is knowing. So knowing that a five-year-old's life is all about the now, I can trust that when her ball rolls out onto the street, she is going to run after it. Now, as a Parent-Guardian, I can be trusted.

A more complex example: If you are in an intimate relationship with somebody who is not feeling fulfilled, is it wise for you to trust in her fidelity? Or should you trust in the possibility that she will eventually be seeking fulfillment elsewhere? If you were to choose the latter, it would be based not on knowledge of what will happen, but rather on the knowledge that you *don't know* what will happen. That opens the doorway to talking with your partner about the realities of your relationship, to help assure that everyone's needs are being met. That will help achieve an outcome that works for both of you. Otherwise you could end up saying, "I trusted you; how could you do this to me?"

Now we can expand *Only fools trust* to *Fools act on trust; the wise act on knowing*.

With all the time we spend on guarding against failure and accidents, and trying and choosing, and working on trust issues, can you imagine how much time and energy would be freed up if we could just blot those concerns out of our reality? The good news is that it's not hard because we create our own realities. The more we immerse ourselves in the Guardian Way the more foreign—even distasteful—those old preoccupations become. Sometimes when I'm with a person who is so victimized or confused that it saps his vital energy, I nearly come to tears as I realize how different life could be for him, only if...

Chapter 10 Citations

1 Pali Lee and Koko Willis, *Tales from the Night Rainbow* (Honolulu: Night Rainbow, 1988), 46.

2 *Oberpfälzische Blätter für Sonn* (Böes, 1877), 27.

3 Margaret Mead, *Some Personal Views* (London: Angus and Robertson, 1979), 122.

CHAPTER 11

SPRINGING THE PATTERN TRAP

If anything is the antithesis of Guardian Consciousness, it is predictability. It makes us vulnerable because we become easy to read. We can be tracked to our destination without having to be followed. If someone watches what we do for a couple of days, she could pretty accurately predict what we do every day.

What makes us even more vulnerable is that someone can easily learn *how* we do things. Even if we change up our routine, and even our location, the person who observed us will be able to accurately predict how we adapt and adjust.

We become vulnerable not only because our actions are pre-dictable, but because of our predictable *reactions*. If someone knows he can get me steaming mad by telling me my mother wears Army boots, he has control over me any time he wants to exercise it.

Our behavioral patterns make us not only vulnerable, but also unreliable. They severely limit our abilities to be fully present, adjust to changing situations, and function to our full potential in serving our people. Instead, we act like programmed robots.

We tend to relegate ourselves to lives of monotony and rou-tine. We are limited not by our potential, but by our program-ming. A Dog living out her days at the end of a chain will never realize her capacity to live a fulfilling life. Sometimes we are no better off, even though our chain is invisible. Looking from the perspective of our Guardian motto *Only actions speak,* if we act like a Dog on a chain, we are one.

89

In this chapter, we're going to break that chain of monotony. We'll discover the way to become the spontaneous, infinitely adaptable beings that we already are. This is not only going to increase our performance levels beyond what we are now able to conceive, but it will also allow us to truly live, rather than merely exist. If you follow the training protocols, the day will come when you will not know your old self. Your friends and loved ones will beg you for some of the same magic potion that you took. Yet as eye-opening as that sounds, it is not my prime motivation here—Guardian Training is my motivation. In order to develop into helpful servants of the people and effective Protectors of the Earth, *we have to start by opening the gateway to our tremendous abilities.* Before we accomplish this, our abilities lie dormant behind knee-jerk reactions and tired, old movement patterns that would put anyone to sleep who could stand to watch us for half a day.

In this Training, we are going to be turned inside out and rattled to the point that at times, we'll wish we never questioned our dumbed-down lives. Those who have the courage to proceed are on the cusp of entering a world that we can now only begin to envision.

Opening the Gate to Our Full Potential

Rather than just talk in theory, I'll show you how it's done. We're going to drop in on a Guardian Training session at the Teaching Drum Outdoor School. Here is the transcription of a workshop with Trainees, probably like you, learning how to break patterns and unleash their inner Guardians.

Tamarack: What do you know about patterned behaviors?

Trainee: They're hard to break.

Tamarack: Why?

Trainee: Because every time we enact the pattern, we're getting more used to it and the more difficult it is to break.

Tamarack: That's one reason. What we are doing is wiring our brain to function that way. When training for a sport, you keep repeating the same movements, until you start doing them spontaneously. The same is true with our mental patterns. The more often we engage with them, the stronger the connections, which are called neural synapses.

Whatever we do either reinforces that synapse or breaks it down and creates a new synapse. This means that you're either further entrenching your pattern or you're breaking it to establish a new one. This is the key to change. What's another reason we keep re-enacting our patterns?

Trainee: It's easier to stay in an old pattern than to develop a new one.

Tamarack: Why is it easier?

Trainee: Because I don't have to think about what I do. And maybe it worked before, so the pattern is useful.

Tamarack: Okay, but there's still a more basic reason.

Trainee: I can do something else at the same time.

Tamarack: That's it! It frees up your brain. If you didn't have the patterned behaviors down to drive a car, you'd have to shift your focus between steering, braking, signaling, and so on, so you would not be attentive to what's happening on the road. We develop driving patterns, and other patterns, so that we can multitask and focus on the things that call for more attention.

We have an amazing mental capacity, but our brains are not nearly as capable as we think they are. That's why we are creatures of habit and pattern—roughly 95 percent of what we do is based on pattern. We are not rational-intellectual creatures; we are creatures of habit and pattern.

This is why some people have such a hard time healing and changing their lives. They think it's mind over matter. Why doesn't it work?

Trainee: Because you're going to keep falling back in that old pattern.

Tamarack: Right. Changing my patterns is the only way I can change myself. Change my behavior and I change my relationships. It's the only thing that can transform me from being victimized to being empowered.

At that point in the workshop, I gave the trainee the seven-step method for breaking patterns:

Step 1: Identify the pattern.
Step 2: Commit myself to changing it.
Step 3: Describe my pattern to those close to me.
Step 4: Ask for their commitment to help me change it.
Step 5: Create a new pattern.
Step 6: Enact the new pattern *every time* the old one comes up.
Step 7: Do it immediately. The quicker the replacement pattern is applied, the more likely it is to stick.

Addressing the Small Stuff

Escaping from the major behavioral patterns that keep us dumbed-down and dysfunctional is essential to becoming a fully functioning Guardian—not to mention being able to revel in the joy of being a fully functioning Human, living as we are intended to live. However, we are much more than our behavioral patterns.

I just stated that around 95 percent of all that we say, do, think, and feel is pattern-based.[1] Our relationship patterns are a significant share of that; but as you know, we are more than what we share with others. Every time we take a step, open a door, or flick a light switch, we enact a pattern. Review your last fifteen minutes, and I bet you'll be able to fill a page with your patterned actions and responses—and you still wouldn't have gotten them all. Go ahead. Pull out a piece of paper and prepare to be amazed by how little your conscious mind is actually involved in your moment-to-moment functioning. Here are some common examples:

- Answering the phone the same way nearly every time
- Checking the same websites in the same sequence when you go online
- Using the same stall in the bathroom at work
- Having the same drink every day on break
- Holding your sandwich with the same hand every time
- Tuning into the same radio station
- Tying the same shoe first
- Stepping into the shower with the same foot
- Brushing your teeth in the same sequence

Some benefits to these routine, patterned behaviors:

1. They are established and unconscious, which assures that we repeat what has worked consistently for us in the past.

2. They free the mind to do other things.

There is only one glitch: Civilized life. Most of us live in environments that are largely stable and unchanging, and therefore we have routines that are largely stable and unchanging. This environment leads to patterned behaviors that we did not experience in the pre-Civilized past.

Instead of a routine schedule, we led lives of continual change. Living largely outdoors, we adapted daily to the ever-changing weather. Tasks varied depending on what was needed. One day we might be hunting, and the next day we could be hide tanning, drying berries, gathering firewood, scouting, mentoring a child in some craft, or any of dozens of other activities.

These varied activities kept us present and actively engaged in the means and ends of our existence, both intellectually and emotionally. Our daily lives concurrently consisted of training for mental acuity, adaptability, and spontaneity.

No extra effort was needed in order to become a fully func-tioning human—which meant living by our wits, serving to our fullest capacity, and enjoying whatever life brought us. The world is different now, but our circumstances do not dictate that we have to be victimized by them. *Our daily lives become routine only because we allow it.* Those who allowed routine in the pre-civilized past were likely eliminated from the gene pool, either by an untimely death or because they were not able to support offspring.

We, on the other hand, can keep breeding no matter how numbed and detached we become.

In order to create a vibrant and ever-changing life that breaks free from humdrum existence, we only need to follow these three guidelines:

1. Take nothing for granted.
2. Make no assumptions.
3. Treat no two things alike.

Do that, and welcome back to humanity! It's a humanity that our ancestors and the Native Peoples would recognize. This small community, I should add, now includes people like you who are awakening to what it is to be Human.

Welcome to a Life of Options

We live in a world that inundates us with options. At any given moment, we can choose to interact with our environment in any way we want. Nothing says we have to eat with our right hand—or even with a fork—or that we have to sit in the same place at every meal. We don't have to dine with the same people, or with anyone at all. When we consider the multitude of options available to us for a task as simple as eating, we instantly transform a daily mind-numbing routine into a spon-taneous and livening training exercise.

It's not about the meal; it's about our minds. We have to just quit reinforcing the neural synapses that we have created throughout a lifetime to keep us on the straight and narrow—a passive, trained, predictable, boring shell of an existence.

Okay, I admit it: *Boring* is a value judgment. Yet there's Truth to my statement. Consider that *misery loves company*. In the lingo of psychology, it would be called *confirmation bias*. What this translates to is that when predictable people get together, they don't see themselves as such because they confirm and strengthen their shared reality. It's their status quo; it's all they know, so they assume it's the norm. Although it might be the norm in our contemporary society, that hardly means it's normal. Take my example of what can be done with a mealtime and start applying it to every aspect of your life, large or small. You have a lot to choose from: 98 percent, remember? The possibilities are nearly endless, which means that the pattern-breaking potential is nearly endless. In Guardian Trainings at the Teaching Drum, it's not unusual for someone to start screaming in ecstasy when she comes to realize what it means to live life consciously. However, pattern breaking is not always fun and easy. In fact, it usually isn't. More often, we hear the agonizing cry of defeat. This is because of what I call the *numb-numb syndrome*. We have a frame of mind (the first numbing factor) that creates synapses that have us performing knee-jerk responses (the second numbing factor).

In order to consciously engage in a behavior or activity— rather than letting the automatic response have its play—we have to override our frame of mind. This is where agony enters. It is not only unfair but inaccurate to call anyone lazy, unmotivated, or incapable—or to see him as being reactive or antagonistic—for struggling to engage in the Training (i.e., to engage in a life consciously lived). This Training often goes against all the patterns of thought and action that we have ever known, which can be quite debilitating.

It Takes a Pack

You've probably heard the saying that *It takes a village to raise a child.* It also takes a village to awaken a Guardian. We need each other's support. We need to hear the success stories. We need to see what it's like to break through and have the willpower to override our old frame of mind—and have the tenacity to stick with it. And we need each other to help catch the patterns we constantly enact but don't recognize because we're so accustomed to them.

The rewards go beyond description. I have yet to meet a person who has regretted her awakening and wants to return to life—or I should say *existence*—as she knew it.

However, there is only one person in a thousand who can do it alone. Nearly all of us need the support and encouragement of our fellow Trainees, and the example and guidance of our Trainers. That is my primary reason for writing this book. You will find a virtual training camp on the Teaching Drum Outdoor School webpage. There you will be able to connect with people in your area or find out how to create a pack, so that you can train with others who have dedicated themselves to transformation. As you read and practice these exercises, you will hear the voices of your peers and the Guardians who have gone before us. They all create an intricate web of history and healing. You are now an integral force in this web.

Chapter 11 Citations

1   Tony Schwartz, "Six Keys to Changing Almost Anything," *Harvard Business Review*, Jan. 17, 2011, https://hbr.org/2011/01/six-keys-to-changing-almost-an.html (accessed April 6, 2020).

CHAPTER 12

CREATING PRESENCE

Our work in the previous chapter helped us break out of automatically resorting to habits and patterns. Here we integrate that work into our everyday lives—and every moment—with an exercise called *Presence Training*. Practiced diligently, the exercise brings us to the point of being ever aware, attuned, and unpredictable. Here are the foundations of Presence Training:

1. **Refrain** from doing the same thing *in the same way* twice or more in a row.

2. **Engage** consciously in whatever the moment places before you. *Make no exceptions.*

It is #2 that typically trips people up. "What if I'm sitting in a waiting room?" someone asked me. "What if I'm driving a boring stretch of freeway?"

Situations like these are ideal for conscious engagement, as it is often at times like these (such as barreling down the highway) that our presence is most necessary. When we allow habit and pattern to lull us into complacency, we become vulnerable. Our senses are no longer as tuned in to our surroundings as they could be, and our response time is reduced.

There is a Guardian saying: *always observing, always serving*. To be fully aware is to keep our people's needs at the forefront. Then, we are ever-ready to spring into service—and to be at our best when we do.

Applying the Exercise

Be inventive. Anything goes, as long as we are engaged in something that keeps us present, attuned to our surroundings. I have yet to find myself in a situation where I could not practice Presence Training, and I'm sure the same will be true for you—if you resolve not to settle for sameness or complacency.

As mundane and repetitive as push-ups, sweeping the floor, or climbing stairs might seem, I find it easy to apply the two Presence Training guidelines to activities such as these. I'll give you two more unusual examples of Presence Training.

I attended a meeting where we all sat in a circle on the floor. Right away, I saw opportunities for a spontaneous Presence Training exercise: catching participants' agitated movements, figuring out the room's air flow from floating dust particles, and assessing the various types of dirt on the carpet. By the end of the meeting, I had a good feel for each participant's emotional state and the room's climate.

I had also amassed a neat little pile of debris from the carpet. I imagined that if all of us participants were in the same Guardian Consciousness, we could have served our hosts by leaving them with a cleaned carpet, while at the same time improving our individual and pack functionality by working as a group on a shared task.

After I came home from the meeting, I found a box of books awaiting me that had been delivered while I was away. I could have easily grabbed the knife I always wear and sliced the box open. Instead, I assessed the situation: a corrugated cardboard box containing perhaps twenty books, secured with fiberglass-reinforced tape. How could I open it without the help of a tool?

Tearing the tape was out of the question, and there was not enough space between the bands of tape to just tear open the cardboard and remove the books. I diligently tore the cardboard in places that loosened the tape enough for me to create an opening big enough to wiggle out one book at a time. Instead of automatically reaching for a tool for the sake of expediency, I transformed this everyday experience into a Presence Training exercise. There are many opportunities like this in our daily lives; we just have to recognize and take advantage of them.

Personal Benefits

Presence Training can enrich our lives. We may suffer fewer injuries because of avoiding potential harm, and we may take advantage of benefits that we would otherwise have missed. The benefits typically include personal fulfillment, good health, longevity, and rapid healing.

I've seen Guardian Training transform people's lives. Some of you may think these are tall claims. Let me give you another example from my life. More than seventy years of age, I give a good share of the credit for my youthful strength and performance level to the continual practice of Presence Training. Yet, a little more than a year ago, I started to lose control of my pelvic muscles. I went to one specialist, then another, and they couldn't help me. The third specialist had a hunch: malfunctioning pelvic-area nervous response, which testing confirmed. On a 1-to-10 scale, my nervous response was down to level 2.

After the second therapy session and consistent follow-through with the recommended at-home exercise (Presence Training in action!), I tested at the top of the chart. In her twenty years of practice, the therapist exclaimed that she had never seen anything close to my speed of recovery. She asked if I could explain why.

I described my diet, lifestyle, and the various exercises I practice. When I got to Presence Training, she stopped me and said, "That's it!" Muscle control, she explained, is all about the mind-body connection. "I only get one or two sessions per week with patients," she said, "and it's up to them to follow through with the at-home exercises. They might do them once or twice a day, but that's it." She thought that because I trained continually, my mind-body connection was already well developed, which made it easy for me to quickly regain control of my pelvic muscles.

Notice that the credit does not go to Presence Training per se, but to the *continual practice of it*. Nowhere more than here is the saying *Training is life and life is training* more fitting. Practicing Presence Training once or twice per day will hardly put a dent in that 98 percent habit-and-pattern figure. We train continually in order to become continually conscious. At that point, practice merges with life and the practice ceases to exist.

A Zen story portrays what life is like after this transformation occurs:

> While talking one day about what it is like to be Awakened, a group of friends came to realize that none of them knew for sure.
>
> "Let us ask the two Nuns sitting under that Tree," one of them suggested.
>
> They approached the Nuns and asked their question.
>
> "Give us experiences from your everyday lives," said one of the Nuns, "and we will do our best to tell you what they would be like if you were Awakened."
>
> "Eating."
>
> "You are the aroma and flavor of the food, which alone fills you."
>
> "Pain."
>
> "Neither pain nor pleasure consumes you, as you dwell between them."
>
> "Exhaustion."
>
> "You let it overtake you, and you feel complete."
>
> "Travel."

"You melt into the creaking and swaying of the carriage, which is an integral part of the new sights and sounds."

"A bug crawling on me."

"It enlivens your senses, which brings you right to the then-and-there."

"Change."

"Rather than it consuming you, you consume it."

"A wandering mind."

"You are there; you are it."

"Self-consciousness."

"There is no fear of abandoning yourself, yet you become each person you are with."

"Being caressed."

"Time transforms into timelessness."

"A clear sky."

"You enter the clarity."

"Lovemaking."

"You are not trembling; the trembling is you."

"An everyday object or person."

"It is as though you are seeing and experiencing it for the first time."

"Something that catches my attention."

"You are spontaneously immersed in the experience."

"I react to someone."

"You stay centered."

As the suggestions trailed off, the friends bowed to the Nuns and left them to the quietude under the Tree.

Ill-preparedness and half-baked plans lead to perpetual cycles of the same. We are creatures of habit and pattern; everything we do either strengthens an already existing pattern or begins the establishment of a new one. In other words, everything we do matters, as it affects not only the present action, but also future actions. This is an important consideration for the Guardian, who is often called to function in times of stress. It is then that we are likely to revert to pre-established patterns. When patterns are solid and functionally based, as well as flexible and adaptable, they can be relied upon to successfully conduct a Mission and serve our people.

CHAPTER 13

SERVING BEYOND EMPATHY

"You just don't understand me."

"I don't know how many times I can say the same thing over and over again."

"I just can't seem to find the right words to express what I'm feeling."

"I get tired of explaining myself all the time. I wish sometimes you could just know what is going on inside of me."

"I bombard you so much with my feelings that I'm afraid you're going to lose touch with the real me."

Have you ever felt any of these ways? Do you know of someone who has? The typical ways we use to gain awareness and empathy for the feelings of another—mirroring, mindful listening, sacred speech, and others—are all useful. At times. However, they can still leave one feeling not fully understood, not fully known, not fully expressed. Why is this?

One reason is that these techniques are just that—techniques. They facilitate respect, openness, and expressiveness, but they do not bridge the gap between self and other, so one can still be left feeling detached, unaccepted, or frustrated. One reason for this discontentment is that getting in touch with someone's feelings is not the same as knowing someone in a deep sense. Feelings are surface. They are the external manifestation of inner dynamic; and feelings cannot be trusted, since they change like the wind. Feelings are malleable and temporary because they are reflective of our intellectual climate, sensory input, knowledge, biases, and preferences, rather than of the deeper self. Also, the language of expressing feelings cannot necessarily be trusted. Words often get in the way, and they can be misinterpreted.

From Self to Other

There is another way to connect with someone that goes beyond speech, beyond listening, and beyond sharing. In fact, sharing can get in the way, much the same as words can get in the way. This other way I refer to takes us deeper than feeling. It involves taking a greater risk than sharing feeling. It is scarier because we leave our ego behind, abandon our cherished beliefs, and step out from behind our boundaries. What we do is *become the other*.

Some of you may be familiar with the technique of *Becoming* your pain or Becoming your feelings, which is Becoming the moment in order to fully know it. I am speaking here of Becoming someone else's pain, someone else's feeling, someone else's moment. This form of Becoming is known by many people, yet it is not widely practiced. It's found in an ancient Buddhist principle that is expressed through this teaching: *In order to know the Buddha, you must become the Buddha.* It is practiced most often in the Zen way by monks and other ascetics because its practice takes knowing meditative silence and the fully developed art of *Shadowing*, which we shall discuss. The Native saying, *You must walk in someone else's moccasins in order to know her*, is another reflection of Becoming. We hear this concept of Becoming expressed in Civilized cultures as well, but usually the meaning has been lost due to our self-protective proclivities.

Becoming is our natural way of knowing and connecting with another. This language beyond words, this feeling beyond feeling, is the way a Wolf knows his mate and the way the trees of a grove know each other. Becoming takes us to a level of rapport beyond understanding and caring. It can touch areas within that are not reachable with words and that can't be accessed by listening or conscious sharing. It is a way of knowing another that is intrinsic, pure, and effortless.

How to Practice Becoming

Let's start with a clear example. If I'm writing a letter to someone and want to know how she might feel upon receiving it, I first become that person and enter a meditative silence. I allow my feelings and my consciousness to be absorbed into that person. I then read the letter as though I were the person receiving it: I allow myself to experience her feelings and reactions.

Another example: When my mate is having a particularly difficult time with something and I want to know what it feels like for her so that I can be truly aware of her reality, we join our hands and together enter a meditative silence. I drop all my fears, prejudices, and preconceptions and allow her to enter me. I let her feelings become mine, I let myself feel her pain, and I even adopt her biases and blind spots. Then we drop hands and I center myself, viewing the world through her eyes and touching life with her feelings.

Sometimes Becoming can be practiced with the other person present, and sometimes the other person can get in the way. In my first example with the letter, if I was feeling at odds with this person and her presence would trigger my reactiveness, I could probably not be in an open and trusting enough place to become that person in her presence. In the second example with my mate, the reverse is true. Because of the level of trust between us, her presence helps me to become her.

Becoming vs. Shadowing

Being as inconspicuous as a shadow is a Guardian skill that has already been mentioned. This ability to move under cover and see without being seen is called *Shadowing*. It is a foundational skill that is intrinsic to the Guardian Way, and it is employed on nearly all Missions. Much of the upcoming training includes the development of Shadowing skills.

Becoming is a progressed form of Shadowing; you might say it is Shadowing perfected, or Shadowing taken to the point where one is no longer the Shadow, but rather the caster of the Shadow. The caster can then look back at the Shadow itself; and in doing so, look back to where she was when the Shadowing initially took place.

When we Shadow, we are in a continual state of stress because we are dwelling in the Shadow, which is the immediate past of the person we are Shadowing. We are constantly trying to catch up with his present. On the other hand, when we Become, we *are* the person, we are the present, we are thinking and feeling and seeing exactly what he does. This allows us to be fully in the moment, since we no longer have anything to strive for or try to achieve—we can just be.

We then have the attitude and perceptiveness necessary to look into the future, to project and anticipate, to thirst and react, just as the person we have Become. By Becoming, then, we have eliminated any distance, time, or stress between self and other.

We are taught to atone for our past and strive for our future, which makes the art of Shadowing difficult for us, and the art of Becoming even more difficult. We are taught that Shadowing, or walking in somebody else's footsteps, is the best we can do, even though that does not bring the deep contentment we naturally crave. This whole-body and whole-mind contentment can be achieved by going one step further and Becoming.

The Inner Process

What we are doing by Becoming is *killing the self*. It is as though we don't exist. More precisely, we forget our self. When one dwells fully in the moment, one becomes the moment and all that is happening in that moment, both within and beyond. Ego ceases to play a role. The dividing line between self and other evaporates. When we kill the self, what we Become is no longer different than us. Self and other are one.

When we have fully Become, we no longer fear hunger or loneliness or death. They are no longer things out there that we are not, so they cease to threaten us. We come to realize that we *are* hunger and loneliness and death. Distraction and denial evaporate also, for we need to be separate from something in order to distract ourselves from it or deny it. When we dwell in the state of Becoming, we no longer feel the compulsion to teach or change, and we no longer have enemies or oppressors. We realize that we are everything that we once thought was our antithesis. We are no longer victims, and we realize that what we thought was hell-bent on destroying us actually *is* us. When I no longer feel separate, I no longer see "other," whether that is another person, a different religion or political system, or another environment. They are all extensions of myself, and I am extensions of them.

From the perspective of Becoming, many realize that the only real change comes from the transformation of self. To try changing another would be going back to being motivated by fear and separation: feeling lonely and vulnerable, acting helpless and oppressed, having our vital energy depleted, and living in a state of stress.

Becoming is what allows the transition from adversity and empathy (which are both the same) to Communion. It's the dwelling in kinship with all life—the animals, plants, fire, air, water, earth, and unseen—that Native People refer to when they say "All My Relations."

Intimidation and Growth

Becoming allows another to know you perhaps better than you consciously know yourself. You may be dominated by your ego, which blocks access to your deeper self. Or the power of your feelings could fog your connection to your deeper self. Another person might not have the same impediments to connection with your deeper self, so he or she could better access it.

Another person Becoming you could help you get in touch with your inner self. In a real sense, that person would be bringing yourself to you.

On the other hand, the thought of someone getting inside you—especially someone you may not care for—could be distasteful at best and intimidating at worst.

Yet for those who are on a journey of self-discovery, feeling repulsed or invaded may be the very reason to invite someone to Become you. As with many of us, your inner self could be quite a different character than the one you wear. The aversion to someone Becoming you might be a subconscious desire to either protect or hide your inner self.

For the Guardian, self-knowing is paramount. For anyone who is in doubt or has psycho-emotional issues, because of what the Becoming process could unveil and catalyze, it is best to undertake Becoming only under the supervision of an appropriate mental health practitioner.

The ability to serve beyond empathy is the ability to serve altruistically. Nurturers serve empathetically, and thus have empathetic perspective. The Guardian has to keep the Greater Good in mind at all times, and Becoming provides for that.

Additionally, a Guardian's ability to Become can be used to unveil hidden motivations, which the Guardian can then pass on to her Elders and fellow Guardians. She might serve an individual by getting in touch with repressed thoughts or feelings that he is not able to express. Whatever the case, it is paramount that the Guardian act honorably with Shadowing, Becoming, and any other skill that she may have.

PART III

THE TRAINING

We Guardians take the saying *Training is life* literally, because how we train is how we live. It reflects strongly in our Mission performance where, under pressure, we intuitively enact our Training. That means more than just applying what we learned—we hold the same mindset and enact the same motions.

It's called *Mind-Muscle Memory.* We are on automatic pilot, reverting to the mechanics and awarenesses of our Training, rather than to current judgment based on what our senses, rationale, and conscience are telling us. On the other hand, if we were to train for routine stimulus-response performance, we would execute a Mission by stimulus-response. It wouldn't matter whether we were relaxed or in a state of dynamic tension, or whether or not we were aware of other possibilities. We would function as methodically and predictably as robots.

We train to rely on Mind-Muscle Memory by consistently approaching varying conditions in the same way, such as stepping over clumps of vegetation rather than on them. On a Mission, we will then—without having to think about it—move stealthily without leaving a trail of broken stems and crushed leaves.

The traditional Guardian trains hard. Yet by the standard definition of the term *training—the process of* learning the skills you need to do a particular job or activity[1]—we would more properly call it *un-training*. We deconstruct the systematic nature of

109

customary training, with its prescribed format and repetition, by emphasizing spontaneity and demanding inventiveness. The constant injection of the unexpected allows the trained Guardian to enact intuitive motions while remaining flexible during an ever-changing Mission.

Developing Mind-Muscle Memory makes Guardian Training fit seamlessly into our lives—and makes a Mission flow as smoothly as a training.

CHAPTER 14

FIRST, THE FUEL

A car can function at peak capacity only if it's given the fuel designed for it—if that fuel is clean and of high quality. The same is true of us Humans, and even more so for those called to be Guardians since we can settle for nothing less than serving our people and our Mother-Planet to the utmost of our ability.

The mind-body connection is an important consideration for the Guardian, who lives by the precept *As goes the body, so goes the mind*, and vice versa. Physical tone, acuteness, and dexterity run a direct parallel with mental tone, acuteness, and dexterity. Physical energy is mental energy, and physical sloth is mental sloth. For the sake of overall performance, the importance of diet cannot be overemphasized.

The question, then, is "What is the proper diet for us?" The debate rages on, with the bestseller lists bursting with books promising that eating this food or avoiding that food leads to a better life. With all the contradicting advice, it's hard to know which food regimen to follow.

Yet if we look back to the diets of ancient Humans and our pre-Civilized ancestors, we find the dietary practices with which we evolved and that made us who we are today. In other words, we find the diet we were made for. It is the diet of most of the world's hunter-gatherers, both past and present. They need to function optimally in order to survive, so natural selection helps form their diet and determine ideal food ratios.

For the sake of clarity, I will refer to our ancestral diet and optimal approach to nutrition as the *Guardian Diet*. Variations of the Guardian Diet, which have become quite popular, go by many names: low-carb, Atkins, Dukan, South Beach, ketogenic, and Paleo. Following is a full description of the Guardian Diet and how to incorporate it into your life.

The Benefits

Sustained Energy

The more you cut carbohydrates, the more you gain from the Guardian Diet. One primary benefit of the diet is that instead of relying on carbohydrates for energy, your body's new energy source is fat. The rollercoaster physical and emotional energy peaks and valleys typical of people on carbohydrate-based diets are replaced by the steady, sustained energy that comes from burning fat.

People who begin this diet are often amazed at their consistent energy level. Many of them were hypoglycemic, which means that their blood sugar levels dropped between meals, causing them to become tired, lightheaded, and low-energy. In extreme cases of hypoglycemia, people's hearts race and they can sweat, tremble, and become nauseous, confused, and anxious.

I have the same stable energy flow throughout the morning whether or not I eat breakfast, and I can fast the entire day and perform better than if I were eating. Preparing, eating, and digesting food takes time, energy, and focus, which is freed up for other things when I fast. The reason is that I enter a state called *ketosis*, in which the body uses stored body fat for sustained energy, instead of relying on calories that come from eating carbs.

For Maximum Benefit from Ketosis,

Go twelve or more hours every day without eating. This is easily achieved by having your evening meal a few hours before going to bed, then waiting a couple of hours after you wake for breakfast.

Conditioning through Fasting

The Guardian Diet causes changes in the body that mimic fasting, which is why people lose surplus weight even though they consume a high quantity of fat, which is more than twice as dense in calories as carbohydrates.

The beauty of this diet is that you receive many of the benefits of fasting without feeling hungry. Other less obvious benefits are changes in the brain that drastically reduce the aging process. In your elder years, you can expect to perform better on a memory test than young adults subsisting on a normal diet. Along with feeling younger than you do now, you will be smarter, quicker, and maintain your ideal weight perhaps for the first time in your adult life.

Yet more can be gained from fasting in addition to the diet, particularly regarding metabolic efficiency, overall stamina, and immune system function. I recommend fasting roughly one day per week, beginning after the evening meal the day prior, and concluding with breakfast the following day. Consume only water during the fast.

Rather than creating a routine (antithetical to the Guardian Way) by designating a particular day, choose a day when you are particularly busy, when you want to function at your peak, or when you are traveling and don't have access to good food.

A three-day fast every one to three months further hones the system. In order to be more effective than a one-day fast, a fast must be a minimum of three days in duration because full ketosis does not kick in until the third day.

Additional Advantages

The saying *You are what you eat* rings true with the Guardian Diet. It supports optimal:

- Brain function
- Emotional well-being
- Physical strength
- Coordination
- Sensory acuity
- Immune system functioning
- Cardiovascular health (cholesterol, blood pressure, heart)
- Weight (you automatically gain or lose to reach your ideal weight)
- Longevity

Dietary Components

Our ancestors ate what was available to them, which varied from season to season. The same is true of contemporary hunter-gatherers. You can get an intimate view of what that is like in my book *Fat Moons and Hunger Moons: The Turn of the Seasons for Northwoods Natives.*

In essence, the Guardian Diet is comprised of foods that have:

- High fat
- High fiber
- Moderate levels of protein
- Minimal carbohydrates

When we hear the word *diet*, most of us assume right away that it will include restrictions on what we eat. One reason for our assumptions is that we come from a *culture of scarcity*, which is based on the premise that we need more to be secure and happy, and we must compete with each other in order to get it.

The Guardian Way, along with the lifeways of Native Peoples, is rooted in the *culture of abundance*, where the Great Mother provides for all her children. Sharing is practiced rather than hoarding, and joy comes more from the qualitative than quantitative aspects of life.

When we approach a new way of eating from the culture of abundance perspective, we are more likely to get excited about the wide range of new foods available to us than to lament what we can no longer eat. If the diet is based on sound nutritional principles, we will be further delighted by the health benefits, rather than bemoaning the loss of the foods we are giving up. We might also realize that from an objective perspective, there are always restrictions on what we eat based on what is available at the moment, our beliefs around food, what we can afford, and so on.

With that in mind, here are the foods to incorporate and skip in formulating your version of the Guardian Diet:

Foods to Include

- **Animal protein:** mostly fish, along with red meat, poultry, eggs
- **Above-ground vegetables:** leafy greens, cauliflower, broccoli, zucchini
- **Fats:** olive, nut, coconut, and avocado oils, avocados, grass-fed animal fat; small amounts of dairy fat in the form of butter, pure cream, and hard cheeses made from grass-fed animal milk
- **Seeds and nuts:** all tree nuts (not peanuts, which are legumes) and seeds, such as sunflower, sesame, pumpkin, and chia
- **Berries:** blueberries, blackberries, raspberries, cranberries

Foods to Avoid

- **Legumes:** beans, peas, peanuts
- **Grains:** wheat, rice, corn, cereal, granola, all grain-based bread and baked goods
- **Tubers:** yams, beets, potatoes, turnips
- **Most fruit:** including bananas, oranges, and apples
- **Sugar:** cane sugar, maple syrup, honey, any sweet concentrate from fruit or plant juices
- **Starchy vegetables:** squash, pumpkin
- **Dairy:** all except occasional butter and cream

What to Drink and Not Drink

- **Water:** the only acceptable between-meal drink because it allows the digestive system to complete its process and rest for the next meal
- **Fruit and vegetable juices:** containing all the pulp and no added liquid, and only as meal components or meals in themselves
- **Stimulant drinks:** coffee, other caffeinated beverages, and energy drinks are not to be consumed under any circumstance

Go Organic

The quality of what you eat is just as important as the food itself. Base your diet on organic and wild foods as much as possible. They are the most nutrient rich, the least stressful to the immune system, and the lowest in toxicity.

Meal Planning

The main meal of the day for an active person consists of a ratio of one-third fat to two-thirds protein, along with all the non-starchy vegetables and leafy greens she would like. If the protein is fatty, it counts for both protein and fat. Other meals can consist of nuts (which are high in fat), berries, and vegetables made in any way you choose (raw, steamed, stir-fried, or in salads). Fat can be easily incorporated with vegetables in the form of oils, avocados, and nuts.

Here are additional meal planning and consumption guidelines:

- Fruit is best eaten alone, though nuts can be added. Many people do best with fruit first thing in the morning.

- Eat the protein portion of your meal first to stimulate production of the hydrochloric acid needed to digest it.

- Protein typically is needed just once per day, preferably with the evening meal since growth and regeneration occur at night during sleep.

- Eat slowly and chew well to gain the full nutrient benefit from your food.

- Don't drink anything one-half hour before, during, or two hours after meals, so as not to dilute digestive acids and enzymes.

What If I Crave Off-Diet Foods?

Don't worry about being a purist. With the Guardian Training and this diet, you're going to be in such good shape that you can treat yourself now and then and it won't hurt you.

How to Transition to the Guardian Diet

Intestinal flora is the community of bacteria that live symbiotically in the small intestine to help digest the food we eat. The species and number of bacteria are determined by the type and quantity of foods we eat, and by how we eat. For optimal digestion and health, we need an intestinal flora community that matches our diet.

When we change diets, our intestinal flora needs time to adjust. Otherwise, we could suffer the symptoms of poor digestion, such as bloating, gas, cramps, diarrhea, and reduced nutrient uptake. When someone switches to the Guardian Diet, I recommend this six-day transition that allows the intestinal flora to die back, then gradually rebuild to accommodate the new diet:

Day one: Fast, from the previous evening to the next day's breakfast. Consume just water.

Day two: Eat only steamed green vegetables, with nothing added.

Day three: Add fat or oil to your steamed or raw vegetables.

Day four: Add animal protein, starting with fish, to the evening meal.

Day five: Add nuts and eggs.

Day six: Add fruit.

Some people are scared off by the Guardian Diet because they think it will be too difficult to follow. It's true that old habits die hard (see Chapter 11); yet when we allow ourselves to fully experience the satisfaction of eating the rich fats, oils, and meats that the body naturally craves—but other sources tell us to avoid—it's doubtful that anyone will look back. The Guardian Diet provides us with a deep satisfaction that comes from the high level of performance we are capable of thanks to the sustained and quality energy we find within.

Chapter 14 Citations

1 *Cambridge Academic Content Dictionary*, s.v. "Training" (Cambridge University Press, 2009).

CHAPTER 15

DEVELOP THE TRAINING MIND

It is commonly believed that one trains to improve performance. That may be true in sports training or in preparing for an exam. The Guardian's prime goal of training is not to succeed, but rather to fully *be*. Guardian exercises then, are designed to develop three aspects of the self:

- Awareness
- Adaptability
- The ability to maintain centeredness in Chaos

Any success—or failure—comes as a byproduct of being and is of secondary importance to being. Success at the expense of centeredness is failure. The ability to fully *be* is the pinnacle of Guardian attainment, whether or not a Mission is ever undertaken. This approach is called *the Training Mind*.

The following story illustrates how the Training Mind makes training by example look like something other than it is. It is the most demanding type of training, and because of that I consider it to be the most effective. Remember this: *stealth in training, stealth in being*. When we engage in training that doesn't look like training, we can always be in training, ready to respond. That's why we say *training is life and life is training*.

A young man wanted to learn swordsmanship only from a sworder of great renown. When he finally found the Master, he discovered that he no longer took Trainees, as he was of great age and lived alone in a distant wilderness cabin. Yet the

Master saw something unique in the youth that enticed him to open his door.

"Training for what?" thought the youth after he had spent a few days with the Master and had seen no signs of any training. Day after day and week after week, all he was directed to do was fetch water, split wood, cook, and tend the garden. Never was there instruction in the Way of the Sword. "I am ready to quit," he told himself. "I could go anywhere and be a servant for no pay."

At the same time, he had already invested so much time that before leaving, he decided to ask the Master if training might soon begin.

"It already has," came the reply. "We'll see how well you developed your Awareness while fetching and tending."

From then on, the Trainee couldn't turn his back on anything or focus on any task without fear of getting a rap from the Master's stick. Most frustrating was that it seemed to come out of nowhere. The young man lived in constant stress.

Several cycles of the seasons passed before he could sense a fair number of the coming blows and dodge or deflect them.

"He still has learned very little," thought the Master as he went out to the hearth in front of the cabin to cook his vegetables, which is something he seldom did.

The crackle of the fire disguised the Trainee's steps as he stole up and raised his stick to strike the old man stooped over the pot.

As nonchalantly as the Master stirred vegetables with one hand, he flipped the cover of the pot up with his other hand to deflect the stick.

In that moment, the youth was Awakened—everything made sense to him. It was not what he did, but the Training Mind he maintained while doing it, that made all the difference. Fetching wood, cooking vegetables ... any and every task was an essential part of the Training, as it was the only way to learn how to be ever aware, adaptable, and centered. At that moment, he embraced the Way of the Sword, which was kept secret from him by his own actions. For the first time, he could sincerely appreciate the supreme kindness of the venerable Master in training him.

The Myth of Uselessness

As with the youth in the previous story, have you ever felt unproductive, out of sync, or in the way? How often have you gotten books or music that just didn't resonate with you? And what about those knickknacks, tools, or appliances that get in the way more than they serve? Whether we're applying it to people, places, or things, nearly all of us periodically slap on the label *useless*.

The Zen concept of the *thinking-without-thought mind* refers to our limbic process, which is the sensory-feeling center of our minds that does not rate or compare. When we are centered in our thinking-without-thought minds, we can see that labeling something *useless* is no more than a value judgment; the label has nothing to do with inherent value.

I was raised with the saying *One person's trash is another person's treasure*, and from an early age I saw the utility in those words. Yet it's not always what I practice, even though I might spew it out as a practical ideal. In the next breath, I might judge something *useless,* so it would appear as though I am a hypocrite.

That would be an accurate judgment if it were the same voice speaking in these two situations; however, it's my ego doing the assessing and my thinking-without-thought mind seeing the inherent value in all things. The two don't use the same wavelength to communicate: The ego commands word-based language, and the thinking-without-thought mind functions by feeling, intuition, and deep memory.

When we practice the art of remaining in the state of awareness that allows us to see the inherent value in all things, we naturally treat everything and everybody with honor and respect.

We don't waste, we don't criticize, and we don't neglect. We maintain things, we put things away, and we reach out to help satisfy other people's needs.

The uselessness label is just a trick of the ego to keep *self* at the center of attention. It works by diminishing *other* to create a false sense of security and value. Our intrinsic self knows that everything exists for a reason, which gives it inherent value. Whether or not we are capable of consciously recognizing this has nothing to do with the fact that it is the way of things.

Now all that's left to do is strike the word *useless* from our vocabulary, and we have set the stage for entering the Training Mind.

Training on the Edge of Propriety

The rest of the chapter is devoted to a five-step process for reestablishing Training Mind consciousness. Notice the momentum gaining with each step; you are doing nothing more than returning to the way your mind is designed to function. Notice that each step describes a primary characteristic of a young child before she is taught otherwise.

As the Trainee learned in this chapter's opening story, you can make stealth training an integral part of your every thought and action by sequentially incorporating the following practices.

First: Welcome Problems

We thrive on glitches, snags, and complications—they are the incentives behind all inspirations. Every Mission is a problem, and a Mission must be approached as such or we will not engage our creative and deductive energies to the utmost. In our hunter-gatherer past, we continually faced problems, such as how to stay safe and where to find our next meal. We evolved to solve these problems in order to survive. Our brains are designed entirely for problem solving; so to fully engage our brains, we need to feed them problems.

Second: Avoid the Camp Dog Syndrome

What does a dog do when he is well fed and has no cares or responsibilities? He hangs around camp, gets up to stretch once in a while, lays down to take a nap, goes to relieve himself, then comes back and lays around some more. We do the same when we're satiated, our needs are provided for, and we don't have anything in particular that we need to do.

As anyone knows who works with hunting dogs or other performing animals, they function at their peak when they are hungry. The same is true with wild animals. The wolves I lived with were alert, inquisitive, and raring to go just before we went out on a hunt because they had good reason to be—a hearty appetite. When they had full bellies, their only interest was to find a sunny spot and stretch out for a nap.

Same is true for us, as we are essentially predators, just like Wolves. Intellectually, emotionally, or gastro-intestinally, we function best when we are motivated by our various hungers.

Third: Inject Mischief

What could be more engaging than mischief? It brings in the unexpected, the element of surprise, and the need to be adaptable and innovative. When engaged in mischief, we need to keep our senses keen and our minds razor-sharp, in order to be *cunning* and *deceptive,* which are the signature characteristics of mischief. Plus, mischief is just plain fun! While mischief can be useful as a training technique, there is no place for it on a Mission. This may sound contradictory; however, any mischief on a Mission increases the odds of failure, for these reasons:

- A small error in judgment can have large repercussions.
- All decisions need to be made conservatively, allowing for a wide margin of error.
- Mischief often involves split-second decisions, surprise, and unnecessary movement, all of which accentuate

training. Yet, at the same time, they increase the risk of exposure, misjudgment, and pack disjointedness.

Here are two stories to demonstrate:

A Nun walked by a man sitting alone in the village square with a vacant look on his face. "Is there anything you need?" the Nun asked.

"The trouble is, I don't need anything," replied the man. "I have a beautiful family, I have wealth and position, and I have a fat belly. When it comes down to it, I have no reason to move, as all my needs and wants are met."

"Oh, look at the beautiful Bird in that Tree behind you!" exclaimed the Nun.

When the man turned to look, the Nun snatched up the man's satchel, which obviously contained items that were important to him. In a wink, she began to dart down the alley between the nearby buildings.

While the Nun was spry, the man was rather portly. He waddled and puffed in an effort to overcome her. The Nun led him off to the far side of the village, then doubled back and laid the satchel down next to his coat where they had been speaking moments before. Then she hid behind some nearby bushes and waited.

Sure enough, the exhausted fellow came dragging back, stooped over to pick up his coat, and shouted out a seldom-heard expletive when he saw what sat beside the coat.

Realizing that he couldn't remember the last time he had so much fun, he burst into a riotous laugh. "Wizard-Nun, if you can hear me," he shouted, "my gratitude for your trickery extends from one end of the Sky to the other! You have danced me out to the stormy edge, and that's just what my life has needed. I bow to you, and again I bow to you."

•••

A young *Seeker* caught a small Bird and wondered how she could use him to raise some mischief. After all, what youth doesn't like pulling a prank now and then?

"I know," she said to herself, "I'll pull a trick on our Elder!"

This was uncharacteristic for a Seeker, as Elders are generally respected and not involved in shenanigans. At the same time, it is a characteristic of youth not to abide by convention.

The Seeker walked up to the venerable woman, who was known for her piercing insight, and said, "Honored Elder, is the Bird I am holding behind my back alive or dead?"

The kindly woman looked upon the girl with a soft smile.

This caused the Seeker some discomfort, so she quickly reconsidered her plan to let the Bird fly if the Elder said "dead," and to quickly break the Bird's neck if the Elder said "alive." Yet her impish Nature won out, and she mentally prepared herself to proceed.

The Elder read the Seeker's game and replied, "You hold the answer in your hands."

Notice how in each story, the type of mischief presented could contribute to a Mission's failure. In the second story, if a wise Elder was not involved, the outcome could have proven fatal.

As shown in the stories, mischief is characterized by errors in judgment and the split-second decisions it encourages. Both are diametrically opposed to the careful planning and execution that form the basis of a successful Mission.

Fourth: Play to Lose

We have been conditioned all our lives to play to win. Winners are rewarded and losers are forgotten. We're taught that the more we win, the better we are and the more acclaim we deserve.

At first, this might seem to be an effective system, as it motivates us and creates heroes for us to emulate. The only problem is that in the long run, it fails. Winners rest on their laurels and set themselves up as targets to be toppled—and they *will* go down. For us Guardians, winning carries another liability: It stymies growth. When I consistently win games, I don't engage to the level I need to keep me learning. This doesn't mean I need to quit the game; It shows that it's time to engage my Training Mind to stealthily create the challenge I need in order to continue evolving. When I find the trial within myself instead of in the game, I'm able to accomplish the following:

- I can challenge myself by creating obstacles and making more complex moves.
- I can incorporate stealth moves to inconspicuously help the other players get ahead.
- When it comes down to either playing well or winning, I can make the best choice for all involved.
- I can stay out of the limelight.
- I can accept "defeat" with grace and be thankful for the teaching.

My recognition will come later when, because of what I have gained by losing in the contemporary sense, I am able to help execute successful Missions for the good and welfare of my people. Still, I don't do any of this for acknowledgement or accolades; rather, I do it to strengthen myself and in turn, strengthen my pack.

The most rigorous training in games comes when we play to lose. When we arrange it so that we are barely losing, it keeps the pressure on the other players to do their best. At the same time, it gives us the best opportunity to hone our skills for dancing the edge of success and failure—which is not an uncommon Mission scenario.

Here is an example: I once nearly fell while balancing on one foot. It brought snickers from a couple of Trainees who witnessed it. They were new to training and didn't realize that I intended to stumble because, more often than not, it meant that I was pushing my edge. Had they known this and looked closely, they would have seen that I was standing on a fist-sized round stone, which made balancing on one foot quite difficult.

Another time I snapped a stick while stealthily approaching one of our wilderness training camps. I was noticed by a couple of fresh Trainees, who let me know by their looks that they didn't think too much of their new instructor's ability. Again I said nothing. I knew that in time they would learn to always look for what does not at first meet the eye. In this case, I deliberately snapped the stick to see if an older Trainee in the vicinity could catch the disturbance and make out my form.

In essence, what we are doing is not playing to win or lose, but playing to train. Winners always end up losing; failure training is winning in ways that are timeless.

Fifth: Avoid the Security Trap

Most of us seek safety and security. That's because we are either not Guardians or we have not awakened to the fact that we are. For the Guardian, safety and security are illusions. As soon as she feels safe, her level of alertness diminishes. She is no longer out on her edge, where life is unpredictable and she continually discovers new things about herself and the world around her. Any Guardian who allows herself the luxury of security and safety creates an illusion. The more secure she feels, the more vulnerable she becomes; the safer she thinks she is, the more she harms herself. It is the Guardian's nature to dwell in an arena of dynamic tension without being in a state of dynamic tension herself, so that she can stay sensitized and responsive. When she becomes her surroundings rather than remaining a shadow of her surroundings, she drifts into a state of security and ceases to be a functional Guardian.

In addition, living in a state of security and safety is boring—even depressing—to the fully actualized Guardian. Her psyche is designed for living with uncertainty, and when she doesn't have it, she goes out to find it.

I suggest returning to this chapter periodically throughout your Training, to review where you can do more to bust the myth of uselessness and incorporate one or more of the steps to reawaken the Training Mind. Don't expect that you'll ever outgrow this chapter. After fifty years of training, I still relish what I gain every time I revisit a step and discover what more I can do to fully grow into my Guardian self.

CHAPTER 16

A PHYSICAL TRAINING PRIMER

Native People do not follow physical exercise regimens that are separate and distinct from their daily lives, and they rarely exercise merely for the sake of exercise. Nor do any other animals I am aware of. So how do those Lions, Eagles, Sharks, and Humans stay in such good shape? Their exercise is a natural component of daily living. Like them, when we are fully engaged in all aspects of our lives, we get exactly the right quantities and qualities of physical, mental, emotional, and sensory exercise that we need to function optimally.

"But what about building muscle mass?" I am sometimes asked. Of all the photos of hunter-gatherers I have studied, I have yet to see an over-muscled or obese individual. Both conditions are liabilities: They reduce stamina, dexterity, and speed, which are vital qualities for the hunt and other activities required to live in Balance with the Earth.

Anthropologists tell us that the human physique is designed for sustained physical activities like distance running and swimming. True to form, contemporary distance runners have the type of physique I commonly find in hunter-gatherers: lean and evenly proportioned, with musculature that is well developed and solid, but does not stand out as anything exceptional.

However, not all endurance events create the ideal physique. "As you look at the runners [going] up from the 100-meter to the marathon," says University of California exercise physiologist Keith Baar, they "are getting progressively smaller. The more

muscle mass you have, the more you have to carry, the less efficient you are." He goes on to say that building bodies for sports
like cycling, rowing, and swimming is difficult "because you're
trying to maintain this big mass while you also build endurance."[1]

"We've evolutionarily been designed to not allow that,"
adds Stephen Seiler, exercise physiologist at the University
of Agder in Kristiansand, Norway. "We're having to develop
these tricks [exercise regimens and special diets] in order to
be able to do that."[2]

Despite contemporary society's idea that bigger is better
when it comes to muscle mass, the opposite is more true: A
slim, toned physique allows us to move faster and longer. Our
ancient ancestors knew it, and now so do we.

What Exercising Says about Us

It is the mark of an idle and affluent society when people have
to seek out exercise. "Our hunter-gatherer ancestors would
have found the idea of exercise for exercise's sake ludicrous,"
says Spencer Wells, head of the National Geographic Society's Human Genome Project.[3] Native and traditional peoples,
just like Native and naturally living animals, stay in shape and
grow in strength and dexterity through daily and periodic
activities such as:

- Chopping wood
- Carrying water, supplies, children
- Gathering and processing foods
- Running down animals
- Seasonal migrations
- Hide tanning
- Shelter building
- Physical play

The more sedentary a people, the more disconnected they
are from the means and ends of their existence, the less often
they do the things their bodies and minds are designed to do,

and the more out of shape they become—both physically and mentally. They are prone to the predatory afflictions that stalk the out-of-shape person, such as cardiovascular disease, diabetes, and chronic depression.

And perhaps even sadder, the sedentary, disconnected person never reaches the full potential of his intrinsic capabilities. The saying *Use it or lose it* rings true here.

The Civilized Person needs to take time out of her day to exercise. An entire industry has evolved, featuring exercise machines and weights in a myriad of types and sizes, exercise clubs and gyms, exercise books and videos, exercise gurus, exercise fields and pools. There are mental exercises, emotional exercises, sensory exercises—even spiritual exercises. And let's not forget taking time to exercise our pets.

There are two things I cringe at paying for: water and exercise. I believe they are our birthright. When we have to buy them, it is a sign that our lives are out of Balance. Isn't it bad enough that we have to plan exercise into our couch-potato lives, without having to pay for it as well?

Exercise and the Guardian

As with Native People, the life of a Guardian involves very little exercise for its own sake. He learns by being—he becomes strong and aware by being strong and aware. His exercise comes through running, swimming, tree climbing, and a host of other activities.

"I run also," you might say, "and I swim." But you probably don't run or swim like a Guardian. Rather than running down a road or path, he goes through the woods or over a boulder-strewn hillside. His run is a dance. He is constantly changing pace and direction: jumping, dodging, darting, stooping, crawling under and over. While running, he's flexing and stretching virtually every part of his body and working nearly every muscle group.

By engaging in a multidimensional activity rather than in structured movement only, the Guardian is growing in mental acuity, sensory perceptiveness, reflex response, overall coordination, observational and decision-making skills, and knowledge of his relationship to his Circle and his Relations.

The Guardian's movement is multifaceted and in the context of a real-life, natural environment. Functioning like a Wolf running through the Woods, the Guardian grows sharp like a Wolf. And like a Wolf, he does not exercise to prepare himself for movement; rather, he moves in his intended way, and that is his exercise. No amount or kind of simulated exercise can equal that.

It's All about Relationship

For me, Communion with The Mother is a sensual and immersive experience. I walk, run, climb, crawl, swim upon Her, for that is how She designed me to know Her. And these are the ways I honor Her; they are my rituals of regard for Her colors and textures, Her smells and the way She feels.

I am seldom drawn to the accouterments that would allow me to move in bigger, faster ways, for I wish to be small and slow with Her. I want to notice the Snail, that I may step over her, and the Mushroom, who offers to be my lunch. I need to smell the scent-mark of Coyote. I have to see the feather intended for my braid. I like to be scratched if I do not belly low enough when searching for Grouse's abandoned nest in the blackberries. So I venture as naked of foot and form as possible, and I use my canoe or skis or bike only when I elect to get somewhere fast and can forestall the gentle process of Communion.

Exercises involving transportation or workout equipment restrict flowing, sinuous, totally involved body movement. When we are an extension of a machine, our movements tend to become mechanical and unidirectional. By focusing on moving the machine, we develop the coordination and musculature to most efficiently operate the machine. With our hands grasping bars or poles and our feet attached to pedals or planks, our motions tend to be simple and repetitive. Certain muscle groups become overdeveloped, while others receive little attention. Our senses and reflexes become finely attuned to the specific band of functioning that supports the operation of the machine.

When our free-flowing form orchestrates our development, its broad-based interactions and complex movements encourage the evolution of overall coordination and adaptability.

The most damaging effect of our use of mechanical equipment for exercise could be losing our primary connection with Earth. The machine becomes our intermediary, our contact point. When our feet no longer touch the Earth and our body no longer moves in the complex and ever-changing dance directed by Her form, we take a step in weaning ourselves from the Mother milk we need to survive. When we traverse groomed and paved trails, we add yet another layer of distance between ourselves and our Mother Earth.

Short and Sweet

Endorphins are the brain's way of encouraging hard work. They are manufactured in the brain, spinal cord, and many other parts of the body. Endorphins are released in response to brain chemicals called neurotransmitters, which are produced by the pituitary gland and the hypothalamus during strenuous exercise, excitement, and orgasm. Acting as analgesics (pain relievers) primarily and sedatives secondarily, they resemble opiates in their abilities to produce analgesia (the absence of pain) and a sense of well-being.

Moderate-intensity aerobic exercise lasting at least twenty to thirty minutes produces the greatest increase of endorphins. These endorphins interact with the receptors in the brain to reduce our perception of pain. The effect plateaus at around twenty to thirty minutes, which corresponds with the time that muscles use up their stored glycogen.

If we were to continue to exercise beyond thirty minutes to exhaustion, our endorphin level would drop dramatically. One test showed that after twelve weeks, one group that bicycled intensely for twenty minutes increased their aerobic capacity as much as the other group that had pedaled leisurely for fifty minutes. Additionally, the twenty-minute group increased their insulin sensitivity by as much as the fifty-minute group.[4]

How Often to Go Aerobic

Every other day is ideal. On rare occasions, it's okay to go five days a week.

Short, high-intensity workouts like weightlifting do not produce endorphins. They are produced by total-body exercises like running, swimming, and active sports. Exercises requiring the holding of a position (such as isometrics, planks, and some kettlebell workouts) put potentially harmful stress on muscles and tendons. In addition, they build *dumb strength*, which is power in the absence of agility and coordination.

Even when sedentary, you can activate muscle groups. Whenever possible, squat or stand instead of sitting. Native People squat regularly, for a variety of reasons. Squatting maintains muscle tone by activating the major muscles of the back, legs, and buttocks. Often there is the option to stand rather than sit, and thanks to current research extolling the benefits of standing,[5] a variety of standing desks are now commercially available.

A Note on Stretching

Indulge in stretching whenever you feel the urge, as it is a natural form of isometric exercise. Yet do not stretch beyond your present physical limits, as you could strain a muscle or tear connective tissue. Instead, stretch passively by placing your arm or leg on something and leaning into or away from it.

Stay Limber

We can tell we are performing well when we are limber and relaxed, tensing just the muscles needed to perform. When we are stressed or unsure of ourselves, we tend to tense up, which interferes with performance and responsiveness.

We also tense up when we focus on movement. It is the inevitable result of repetitive movement training; we know and anticipate our next move, which creates dynamic muscular tension. Most sports, martial arts training, and "relaxation" exercises fall in this category. These activities are based on repetitive movement training because a great deal of planning and pre-staging are necessary in order to be successful in their practice.

Rather than movement training, the Guardian trains *for* movement. He allows movement to be part of the overall flow of an activity, melding movement into the ever-unfolding moment. Remaining present in the moment, he becomes centered in movement—he becomes the movement.

In order for this centeredness-in-movement to happen, all muscles and joints need to remain limber, except for those directly executing the movement. Staying limber is the natural result of living limber. No additional effort or exercises are needed.

Let's take a look at my teachers: our wild animal kin. They either stay limber during a chase or fight, or they die. To learn how to maintain limberness, they don't engage in any exercise regimen other than living an engaged life of immersion in movement. I keep reminding my Trainees: *Forget exercise and think movement.*

The Guardian stays limber and flexible in order to:

- Maintain the flowing body movement necessary to remain invisible.

- Be ready for instant response.

- Keep energy and attention freed up for where and when it is needed.

People argue with me on all three points, either because it goes against their Training or it doesn't make rational sense. "Shouldn't we be in a state of dynamic tension if we want to spring into action?" is one of the most common responses.

In the Civilized World, they are right. When they execute a yoga posture, run a play on the field, or face a sparring opponent, there are many more givens than variables. Planning ahead and tensing the body in preparation for movement may give them an edge.

However, in the Native World, ignorance is knowing, unpreparedness is readiness, and not being focused allows focus. This is the world of the Guardian, where not being intentional serves the greater intent. When we don't concentrate on anything and just give ourselves over to the moment, we become present and intentional by default. Trying to be centered or focused can throw us off course by shifting our concentration onto a desired end, instead of being fully immersed in the moment.

To determine if someone is centered in movement, look for how fluidly the person executes the movement. It should resemble a wave rolling across the water's surface. Someone who is holding herself in a state of tension will execute movements in a deliberate-looking way that often appears mechanical. It's as though she has strung together a series of movements, with jerky stops and starts between them.

Watch a slow-motion video of a bird flying or an adept off-trail runner, and you will see movement without expectation. Body, mind, and emotions are all fluid and open to whatever the moment brings. In this way, we are ready for anything because we are ready for nothing. Without expectations, we are open to whatever unfolds in any moment.

Avoid Repetitive-Motion Training

Repetitive exercises build us up physically and dumb us down mentally. Whenever we exercise out of context with life, such as stretching without the need to stretch or lifting without the need to lift, we take a step toward isolating ourselves from life's rhythms.

Brainless exercises, such as stationary running and weight training, weaken the body/mind connection. This is not to deny their benefits, but merely to state that there are better ways for the Guardian to train. In order to contribute to a Guardian's development, an exercise must meet four criteria:

1. Engages the entire being, both mentally and physically
2. Provides continuous challenge
3. Is non-repetitive
4. Is integrated into the regular flow of life

These four points create a synergistic effect by feeding and fortifying body and mind simultaneously. To tone your body-mind and support your development as a Guardian, avoid any exercise that does not incorporate at least three of the four criteria.

Real Strength

Intensity builds strength, capacity, and energy reserves. Rather than just getting by with the minimum amount of exertion, carry a little extra, chop a little longer, run a little farther, and take the more challenging trail. You'll be glad you did when your strength is put to the test during a Mission.

Training can offer a certain type of strength, which might create the illusion of being strong. Learning a technique can yield a certain type of mastery, which may create the illusion of overall mastery. But when we focus on growing strong in one area, we grow weak in another area. When we focus on a single exercise, technique, system, practice, discipline, or tradition, we become inept in another.

How, then, does one become strong in a well-rounded way—a true Master? The problem arises when we think we are weak and inept and must become strong and masterful to succeed. This is an illusion. We are born strong, with innate ability. The goal is to unlearn rather than to learn, to become again spontaneous and adaptable rather than studied and focused. A Wolf does not study a particular technique or follow a training regimen to learn how to be a hunter—a Wolf plays. We are no different. To not focus on something is to focus. To not believe one is weak and deficient is to be strong and capable. To not want something is to have it. This mindset goes far beyond any physical activity or exercise—it is a way of life.

Chapter 16 Citations

1   Chris Gorski, "Why Olympic Rowers and Runners Have Different Physiques," *Inside Science*, last modified July 31, 2012, https://www.insidescience.org/news/why-olympic-rowers-and-runners-have-different-physiques (accessed October 12, 2019).

2   Ibid.

3   Spencer Wells, *Pandoras Seed: Why the Hunter-Gatherer Holds the Key to Our Survival* (New York: Random House, 2011), 69.

4   Jenna B. Gillen et al., "Twelve Weeks of Sprint Interval Training Improves Indices of Cardiometabolic Health Similar to Traditional Endurance Training Despite a Five-Fold Lower Exercise Volume and Time Commitment," *PLoS One* 11, no. 4 (2016): e0154075. https://doi.org/10.1371/journal.pone.0154075 (accessed April 7, 2020).

5   Shuchi Agarwal, Craig Steinmaus, and Carisa Harris-Adamson, "Sit-Stand Workstations and Impact on Low Back Discomfort: A Systematic Review and Meta-Analysis," *Ergonomics* 61, no. 4 (April 2018): 538-52.

CHAPTER 17

RUNNING AND SWIMMING LIKE A SHADOW

Having gained an understanding of the advantages of raw, un-programmed movement, let's further unpeel the structured conditioning that weds us to routines, so that we can again move intuitively in the flow of the now. We'll then drift as fluidly over the land as a Deer and glide as gracefully through the water as an Otter.

Let's start with the ability that distinguishes us most from all other roaming animals—and that may have contributed the most to the evolution of our species.

Why We Run

We are strange creatures. We started by climbing down out of the trees and, with arms longer than our legs, we hobbled around on our knuckles. Now, with legs longer than our arms, we are one of the planet's master runners. We are capable of running down Horses, Deer, and the swiftest of Antelope. We can run for the entire day without stopping, and on into the next day if need be. How and why did we go from struggling to shuffle over the jungle floor to being the Ascendant Master of the Run?

The transformation happened because we became open-land pack hunters. We probably evolved our pack-hunting behavior from foraging strategies, which were focused on finding and scavenging off the kills of other predators. As we grew in upright stature and bipedal proficiency, we started to hunt our own animals. It is here that we took our great leap forward as a species.

Two evolutionary features that no other animal utilized like we did made us the Great Hunter: endurance and coordination. Our lung capacity increased dramatically. We developed a method of bipedal locomotion and fat reserves to fuel the run that no other animal had.

Most prey animals are known for their speed on the takeoff. Whether it is flying, swimming, or running, they need to set off rapidly to avoid being attacked and eaten. Most predators use the same strategy: a burst of speed to quickly catch their prey or else they're out of luck. A predator's ability to capture prey is generally dependent upon a combination of speed and agility. If she doesn't nab her prey on the first try, it's out of sight, out of mind, and she's off to find another meal.

We Humans have developed quite another hunting strategy, based on endurance rather than speed. When I stated that we could outrun a Horse, I'm sure many of you thought, "That's ridiculous!" Anyone who has seen a Horse at full gallop would consider my statement preposterous, right?

You would only think that if you didn't follow the Horse on her run.

Horses and many prey animals evolved a tremendous capacity to shoot off the line to escape becoming the feast for a predator. However, if we were to follow that Horse, we would see that she is not able to sustain that full gallop for long. She will become winded and run out of energy quickly.

Here is where our endurance comes in. We may not be fast runners, but we can go and go, and we can run that Horse—and virtually every other fleet-footed animal—right into the ground with our unceasing persistence. How is that possible?

1. **Tracking Ability**. Humans are uniquely capable of reading signs left by the animal, even though he is out of

sight—and even long gone. This ability allows us to use our endurance to keep on the trail of the animal and literally run him down.

2. **Musculature.** We have a muscular structure highly evolved for distance running. Even though a Horse is well-muscled for running, he carries his big-barreled gut along with him, which he needs in order to consume, digest, and extract enough nutrients from low-energy plant matter. We, on the other hand, fuel ourselves with high-energy meat and fat. This allows us to have relatively small guts in relation to our musculature. Compare the muscle mass of a Horse's legs to his gut mass, then do the same with us. You will see a significant difference. This gives us an advantage when it comes to endurance running.

3. **Mental Capacity.** The longer the hunt and the more distance covered, the more the hunt needs to be coordinated. When a prey animal falls out of sight, we can no longer rely upon sensory input, so we must conceptualize the situation. This ability, called *envisioning,* was the catalyst for ancient Humans evolving increased mental capacity. We needed the extra deductive ability to interpret the signs left behind by the animal in order to trail her.

We didn't stop there. With the tool of envisioning, we increased both the efficiency and the success rate of the hunt. We could take shortcuts to ambush animals who used circling back as an escape strategy, and we could lie in wait for an animal without having to first flush her. Aside from the hunt itself, we developed the unique ability to learn tracking and hunting strategies from the experiences of others through storytelling.

This combination of skills led to our use of traps and snares, helping us multiply our efforts by giving us the ability to be elsewhere during the kill. We could set a number of traps and have them do the work for us.

Running for Conditioning

No other form of exercise conditions us like running. Along with benefiting our musculoskeletal system, running strengthens our cardiovascular, respiratory, nervous, and glandular systems. In addition, running stimulates the release of endorphins, which gives us increased sensory acuity and reserve energy.

In order to fully benefit from the run, we need to take it beyond the realm of mere physical exercise. The easiest way to do that is to get off of prepared surfaces. They relegate running to just another repetitive-motion exercise, which if sustained is nearly always harmful to joints and skeletal structure. In addition, there is virtually no mental stimulation or improvement in coordination and reflexes.

Any natural environment will do; the more varied it is, the better. Choose an area where you will need to continually process sensory input to envision where to place your next step. Keeping in touch with trajectory and destination helps to develop a sharp mind and finely attuned senses.

Group running yields even more benefits than running alone. We can simulate our ancestors' coordinated effort of the pack hunt by doing the following:

- Running off trail
- Stepping in each other's footsteps
- Negotiating unfamiliar territory
- Finding a predetermined item or location
- Incorporating a game

Along with the ability to endurance run, the coordinated long-distance hunt is one of the unique skills that guided our evolution to becoming Human. The most distinctive feature of the long-distance hunt is *intelligent running*, which incorporates the skill set I just covered. If we want to fully experience what it is to be Human by becoming highly conscious and amply developing our innate capacities, we can do it most easily with intelligent running.

Following is an entry-level start to intelligent running that can be done just about anywhere. Some Trainees use it as an elite awareness-coordination exercise.

The Egg Dance

1. **Choose an oval or rectangular spot** about two or three body lengths wide and half as long. An egg-shaped area is ideal, with varied elevations and diverse groundcover. You want a variety of things to step over and around, such as stones, tufts of grass, branches, and tree stumps. A couple of trees and boulders thrown into the mix are helpful, as well.

2. **Run around in the oval,** working to step between, rather than on, anything littering the oval. This is to keep your profile low and avoid twisting an ankle—the last thing you want to do on a Mission. When you train this way, it's how you will automatically move on a Mission.

3. **Don't ever repeat the same route.** Keep varying direction and foot placement.

4. **Make your route as challenging as possible,** by side-stepping, backstepping, squeezing between objects, and making abrupt turns.

5. **Start slow.** With physical training, it's most important to first learn to move with finesse and precision. Your speed will gradually pick up on its own, and you will find yourself moving faster and quieter than if you had overexerted yourself in the beginning.

6. **Continue for around twenty minutes,** or until you have physically and mentally exhausted yourself.

I sometimes incorporate a couple of Egg Dances into a regular run. Occasionally an Egg Dance will comprise my entire run, which can be a heavy workout!

Woods Running Anywhere

A Trainee once said to me, "Woods living seems to develop people's bodies in a well-balanced way. But when we don't live in the woods, what can best replace that tonifying daily activity?"

I answered this question by giving some examples of what I've done. When I lived in Ithaca, New York forty years ago, I would do my "woods running" by incorporating bike racks, railings, hedges, curbs, flowerbeds, landscaping rocks, tipped-over garbage cans, and anything else I came across to add variety and challenge to my urban runs.

One winter around thirty years ago, I lived in an upper-level small apartment and created a "woods run" *in* the apartment by using a step ladder, a vacuum cleaner, furniture, tables, an exercise bike, a laundry basket, and a number of other items lying around as substitutes for fallen trees, brush, and boulders. My workouts in that apartment were nearly as satisfying and inventive as my workouts in the woods.

We should not allow our circumstances to limit us. Limitations are only opportunities in disguise. And besides, the only real limitation is the one we create in our minds.

Bareback Running

With one simple adjustment—taking our shirt off—we can transform our Guardian run into a multi-dimensional exercise with benefits that go beyond the run itself. Running shirtless naturally conditions us to become:

- **More aware of our surroundings**
- **More careful about what we touch and disturb**
- **More in tune with our enlivened senses**
- **Better able to acclimate to changing physical and environmental conditions**

I like to run bareback in all weather conditions except when the temperature drops significantly below freezing. If I'm chilled when I start running, I know I will soon warm up. When I'm concerned about frostbite or becoming so chilled that I won't be able to warm up, I leave my top on until I have generated sufficient heat to safely disrobe.

Intelligent running is the single most beneficial physical Guardian Training exercise. I incorporate it into my daily life by following the motto, *Why walk when you can run?* Whether crossing our campus, going out to the road to get the mail, hiking into our wilderness training camp—or even crossing a mall parking lot—I usually run rather than walk.

Training-wise, the parallel to running in a water environment is swimming. It carries all the benefits of running, and it allows many people with physical impediments that limit their running ability to train. Following is the discrete method of swimming I learned from living and frolicking with water animals.

Stealth Swimming

In my course on *Dolfinning*, I demonstrate how to become one with the water by immersing yourself in it like a Dolphin or an Otter, rather than paddling over the surface like a Duck. With Dolfinning, you can move silently and inconspicuously through the water. When you come up for a breath, you make no more disturbance than a Fish rolling on the surface.

Four principles of Dolfinning:

1. **Do not break the water with either your hands or feet.** It will help you maintain silence and not create waves.

2. **Swim under the surface as much as possible.** When done properly, someone watching you will have no idea where or when you will surface for air. Imagine this worst-case scenario: Someone on the shore or in a boat has a gun and is trying to shoot you. By the time he sees you and swings his weapon in your direction, you've already filled your lungs and are back underwater.

3. **Breathe with your head to the side or face up,** to expose as little of yourself as possible and create a minimum amount of surface disturbance.

4. **Exhale underwater and through your nose.** This keeps your nasal passages clear of water and reduces your surface exposure and breathing time.

To learn Dolfinning by example, as I did, watch other water mammals such as Manatees, Seals, Otters, Dolphins, and Whales. If you are not fortunate enough to live near them, video footage is available online. Watch how the animals move sinuously with their whole bodies, rather than just using their flippers, arms, or legs.

Pay special attention to how relaxed water mammals appear. If there is any secret to becoming one with the water, it's tranquility. Here is where to begin your course in water relaxation:

1. **In thigh-deep water, take a deep breath** and float face-down in the water.

2. **Slowly exhale through your nose** and allow yourself to sink to the bottom. If you don't sink, swim to the bottom in the gentlest way possible. Use your whole body in synchronized motion rather than just your arms or legs.

3. **When you need to take a breath, come to the surface** in the same slow, graceful way in which you descended. You should have completely exhaled by the time you reach the surface. Now, turn your head to catch a breath, filling your lungs quickly and exposing as little of your head and face above the surface as possible. Another option is to roll over on your back as you rise, so that you only have to break the surface with your mouth to catch a breath. For some people, this is more difficult than staying belly-down and turning the head to catch a breath. If this is the case for you, become adept at the belly-down method first, then progress to the belly-up method.

4. **Repeat Steps 1, 2, 3,** taking the time to stay relaxed and move like a water mammal. Spend as much time with this exercise as you like, gradually increasing the time as your skill improves and comfort level increases.

5. **Once you are thoroughly comfortable, incorporate more movement**, traveling underwater so that you surface to breathe in a different place each time. Gradually increase the distance between the places where you surface. Pay attention to how you are propelling yourself. Experiment with different movements you learn from the water animals.

You are now Dolfinning.

To Improve Your Style

Have someone watch you and give you feedback. Even better, have that person videotape you, so you can watch yourself.

In this learning phase, keep the focus on style. You want your movements to look as graceful and effortless as the motions of an Otter or a Dolphin. Your ability to travel greater distances underwater will come from your improved grace and technique rather than increased effort. This realization is important when performing on a Mission—or simply for the sheer pleasure of being a water mammal for an afternoon—because the less effort you need to expend, the less oxygen you will need, and the longer you'll be able to stay underwater.

Using less oxygen when you swim also reduces the disturbance you make, which decreases the chance you'll be detected. When you're not on a Mission, you'll likely have more fun, especially when you're in a natural body of water; you'll be able to approach fish and other wildlife without causing them to panic and flee. They will simply see you as one of their own rather than as a threat.

For Stealth Canoeing Training

Look up *Solo Canoeing Workshop Teaching Drum Outdoor School online. You'll learn how to paddle silently and efficiently without breaking the surface of the water with your paddle, just like Stealth Swimming.*

Nearly everything the Guardian does is predicated on movement. When you are capable of sustained movement and can effortlessly negotiate varied environments, you free up considerable energy and attention for the task at hand. That's why movement training is central to all Guardian Training Programs, and why I encourage you to take advantage of your daily meanderings by making them trainings.

AT-HOME EXERCISES

Training camp is a high point in nearly every dedicated Guardian's life. Yet we are Guardians as well when we are not at camp. In fact, everyday life training is our backbone; it is where we integrate and apply what we learned at training camp. And everyday life environments are closer to those of a Mission than are a camp's. This is why every Training I conduct starts and ends with at-home exercises.

I'll share a few favorite at-home exercises. These exercises are easy to integrate into the flow of my day, and they never cease to hone my awareness and attunement skills.

Let's start by asking which statement you immediately relate to: "The plate broke," or "I broke the plate." Do you feel uncomfortable with either one of these statements? Does one of them seem dishonest, almost a lie? Would you react differently to one or the other explanation if they were given to you? Before we further explore the issue, I'd like to share a story with you.

While a fellow staff member and I were talking near the entrance to one of our resident buildings, we watched the entry rug get kicked up and wedged in the door nearly every time someone went in or out.

The man I was with said to me, "This rug keeps getting stuck under the door. Do you mind if I move it?" "Are you sure it's the rug that's getting stuck?" I replied. He gave me a quizzical look, as though he couldn't fathom why

I wasn't seeing the obvious. "Straighten out the rug," I suggested, "and then open the door." He was surprised that the door swung easily over the rug, with room to spare.

"How about if we leave the rug there as a training exercise?" I suggested. "If we are in the now and consciously aware of our actions, we'll start lifting our feet and no longer crumple up the rug, so it won't get caught under the door anymore." "Sure," he said, "but why bother if we can just move the rug?" I replied by asking if he could see any fundamental difference between, "that root tripped me" and "that woman stood me up."

"Of course," he said.

"The rug, the root, the woman, it's all the same," I said. "They're all doing something to us—we are their victim. If we keep blaming the rug for getting stuck under the door, we're going to keep blaming women for our relationship issues. However, if we can see our role in messing up the rug and take responsibility for it, the rug will no longer get caught under the door. The same is true in our relationships: If we can take responsibility for our part, we will no longer be screwed over by others." He gave me a long, deep look, then decided to leave the rug in front of the door.

This story lays bare the heart of the following exercise, which I call *The Magic Carpet Exercise.* Learning to be responsible for the rug in the story represents learning to take responsibility for countless other things in our lives. On a Mission, each Guardian has to be a fully functioning member of the pack, which means being Conscious, Aware, and REsponsible (CARE). In order for the Mission to succeed, the pack needs to succeed. Any member who becomes a victim of circumstance weakens the pack, which imperils the Mission.

To keep from becoming victims, we need to create our own circumstances, rather than allowing them to create us. The rug getting stuck under the door becomes an issue imperiling the Mission not because of the rug, but because of me.

The Magic Carpet Exercise

1. **Lay a thin rug where you regularly walk** and would typically ruffle it up.

2. **Walk with CARE**—be Conscious, Aware, and REsponsible.

3. **Move the rug to another location** once you are consistently able to walk over it without ruffling it up, and follow steps 1-2 in the new location.

4. **Lay a few more rugs in different locations** to further test yourself.

Over time, your unconscious shuffling will transform into gingerly stepping. Along with being aware of the rugs, you find yourself noticing so much more around you. Even more amazingly, you will notice yourself becoming more Conscious, Aware, and REsponsible in your relationships.

Sound like a stretch? Not at all. Relationship is relationship, and all relationships manifest the same patterns, no matter what the type. We are creatures of habit and pattern, so we can't help but treat a person the same way we treat a rug. If we externalize on a rug, we are going to externalize on the people in our lives. If we are the numb, hapless victim of a rug, rest assured we are going to be the numb, hapless victim of person after person in our lives.

The reverse is true as well: If we take consistent responsibility for our relationship with the rug, we will—like magic—take consistent responsibility for our relationships with people. We'll start experiencing healthy, joyful, and lasting relationships. We'll become strong, contributing members of our pack, and we will have more flawless Missions. Overall, the quality of our lives will be enriched, thanks to no more than a floppy old rug.

Dance Your Way to Dexterity

One Guardian Training exercise that nearly always raises eyebrows when I suggest it is *dance*. The traditional Malinke people of West Africa say that there is no movement without rhythm. Whether we are stalking an animal in the woods, shadowing our pack on a Mission, or following our partner on the dance floor, we are using the same basic skill set to move with grace and agility.

What makes dance a training exercise is seeing it as such. Be fully present and engaged, and take dance with all the seriousness and emotional abandon that you would any other training, or even a Mission. Remember: Life is training. Here is an excellent and seldom-recognized opportunity to practice this saying.

Some of the benefits of dance training include:

- There is endless variety, which means endless challenge.
- Full attention is required.
- Instant response is necessary.
- It can be practiced almost anywhere.

Nearly any form of dance is suitable for training, as long as it is either free-form or you follow rather than lead. The most effective dances have minimal repetitive movement, so that no two steps are alike.

Polynesian Dance Training

In ancient times, Hula, the chant-dance that served as training in movement and the telling of Guardian stories, was practiced mostly by men. Trainees joined a Halau (Hula School) expecting to die. Training was tough: the raw Earth was their gym and an Elder Guardian was their Kumu (Trainer). They came as balls of clay, to be shaped into individuals worthy of serving their people. The chiefs came to the Halaus to select Hula dancers for Missions. The Halau was a lifelong brotherhood where everyone took care of each other and inspired each other to blossom into the fullness of Guardian Consciousness.[1]

Label-Peeling Exercise

You've already been given a number of exercises that take no extra time or energy. They are essentially upgrades to your normal routines. These activities can be so integrated that someone could watch you and have no idea you were engaged in a training exercise. It would look as though you were doing nothing other than bumbling through your typical routines.

Here's another one of those exercises: peeling a label off of a can. The goal here is to tear the label off from top to bottom or bottom to top in the shortest distance possible. There are only two rules: Do not tear through the glue line, and do not allow any secondary tears to develop. Your tear will progress diagonally up (or down) the label, and it must reach the opposite side of the label before hitting the glue line, or you have to start on the opposite side of the label and work to have your second tear meet the first in order to sever the label. The benefits of this exercise are:

- Another unconscious activity becomes conscious.
- The creative and problem-solving part of the brain is activated.
- It's a fun challenge.
- There's a practical application: peeling other materials such as tree bark and animal skins.

Shame Training

I am one of the few people I know who enjoys being shamed. When I am self-conscious, I have an opportunity to practice functioning with centeredness and perspective, which is a necessary Guardian skill.

However, functioning with centeredness and perspective can be difficult when a person is being:

- Threatened
- Bullied

- Labeled
- Criticized
- Praised
- Or singled out for any other reason

These experiences elicit the same response: feeling destabilized. When we feel challenged as well, our fight-flight mechanism is activated and our center transfers from our Heart-of-Hearts to our ego. We immediately engage in aggressive-defensive tactics.

An aggressive-defensive mindset is detrimental for the Guardian—or for anyone, for that matter. No longer is the Mission all that matters, as we become occupied with taking care of ourselves. We are no longer serving our people. Being shamed is good training for self-conscious scenarios, such as those listed previously, because we can place ourselves in shaming situations with little effort. Here is a list of shame-inducing behaviors that I use on myself and in training:

- Improper or out-of-character dress
- Saying something stupid
- Carrying something appalling
- Asking for something that will trigger a resounding "No!"
- Attempting something in front of others where I know I will fail
- Sharing something meaningful about myself that I've worked to keep secret

Here's how to practice Shame Training:

1. Personalize the list of shame-inducing behaviors by adding other scenarios that are likely to bring you shame.
2. Choose a scenario from the list.
3. Select a location where you are fairly certain your shame response will be triggered.
4. Increase your vulnerability by recalling past situations similar to the one you are orchestrating.

5. When you are triggered, wallow in your self-conscious misery.

6. At the same time, bring yourself to centeredness and perspective by realizing that your shame is not you, and that you are on a Greater Mission, whether it is this training or in service.

7. Engage in this training periodically, using as wide a variety of scenarios as work for you.

The more you practice, the easier you will be able to maintain composure and a sense of presence on a Mission when the unexpected self-conscious moment arises.

Close Your Eyes and Point

The title of this exercise is typically one of the first things Trainees hear from me when they all meet for the first time. It's true during training as well: We usually meet outside in a forest clearing, and the first thing I do is instruct the Trainees, "Close your eyes and point [in the direction from which the wind is coming]."

Sometimes the results are comical—especially when the pack covers each of the cardinal directions. Yet this seemingly simple exercise bears great significance: It is a metaphor for whether or not the pack is of one voice, and it indicates how connected they are with the Greater Circle, which includes the weather, a sense of direction, and the activities of our animal neighbors.

The Trainees quickly learn that the first thing to do when waking up—even before they relieve themselves—is to ground themselves in their surroundings by checking the weather. This means stepping outside and physically experiencing the new day, whether it is cool raindrops on their shoulders or the first rays of the sun on their backs.

The elite Guardian can glean information from her surroundings at a glance. Air temperature, humidity, amount of light, and type of cloud cover tell her immediately what the weather was overnight and what is coming later in the day. Intrinsic to these observations are the strength and direction of the wind.

Trainees learn to pause and look directly overhead to determine the direction the clouds are moving. Checking the clouds in any direction other than overhead gives a distorted perception of their direction of movement. The Trainee soon learns that wind direction at ground level cannot be trusted, as it is influenced by nearby hills, trees, bodies of water, and variations in ground temperature.

Without looking up, the attuned Guardian can tell you at any time of day not only the wind direction, but the prevailing weather pattern and what kind of weather to expect in the near future.

In and of itself, attuning to the weather is a valuable training exercise. It sharpens the senses and develops intuitive abilities, along with creating a feeling of centeredness. Yet this seemingly simple practice has several important implications:

1. **Weather patterns need to be considered** when planning Missions. Is it going to rain or snow? Will we have cloud cover or moonlight? How will the temperature affect the Mission?

2. **Orienteering is wind-related**, especially when it is cloudy and long distances are being covered. When everyone in the pack knows the wind direction, they can each move independently and maintain a sense of direction without having to stay in direct contact with other pack members. Just as importantly, they can trust in each other's ability to do the same. This helps to ensure invisibility because there are no signals to intercept, so a pack member will not betray the whereabouts of any other member.

3. **Scent and sound drift are affected by wind direction.** If there are Dogs in the area, it is important to stay downwind from them. No matter how silently I move, a dog could pick up my scent and discover me.

4. **Scent tracking can play a role** in some Missions. An intruder's camp can be found by detecting the odor of its campfire smoke. The wind direction then tells the direction in which the camp lies. Sound can be used similarly, as sound travels easily with the wind and gets muffled when it bucks the wind.

5. **Stealth is a major factor** when it comes to wind speed and direction, for the following reasons:

▪ A Mission camp needs to be disguised both scent-wise and sound-wise. This is best accomplished when it is located downwind from possible sources of detection.

▪ All movement creates sound, so even when we are silent, we can potentially be heard. The stronger the wind, the easier it is to maintain invisibility.

▪ If the wind dies down during the Mission, the pack could suddenly be detected. So here again, forecasting is important.

▪ Wind direction helps determine the direction of approach, escape routes, and rendezvous sites.

Bob Dylan said, "You don't need a weatherman to know which way the wind blows."[2] A Trainee who relies on the weatherman not only stunts his growth, but also takes the fun out of training. And let's not forget how woefully inaccurate weather forecasters can be when it comes to local conditions. We can't settle for anything other than precision; less than that could cost a Mission.

First thing every morning, keep your eyes closed and absorb what is going on in your immediate environment. Is the temperature comfortable? Is there a breeze coming through the open window in your bedroom? Is the air fresh, humid, or stale? Taking this time in the morning will make you more present and center you for the rest of the day.

After practicing this for a while, you will find that you wake up and know intuitively what is happening in your environment in that moment. You won't have to wait for a cloud to float overhead—you'll simply know.

Cracking Nuts for Awareness

For this exercise, you'll need a bag of in-the-shell English walnuts. Your Mission is to crack them with nothing but your hands. I'll give you three clues to get you started:

- You can use your hand either as a hammer or a nutcracker. It's fine to use both hands if necessary.

- Every nut has a soft spot, and the awareness training comes in finding how to apply your energy in the most efficient way to that soft spot so that you can crack the nut.

- Do the exercise hungry, and resolve to eat only what you crack. This will sharpen your senses and increase your performance level.

Wear gloves if you have soft or sensitive skin.

For those of you with a lot of physical strength, don't just muscle your way through this exercise. For the fully functioning Guardian, brawn is seldom a substitute for brains. More often, as with this exercise, brawn gets in the way by stymying the development of other faculties. On a Mission, the adrenaline flow required to fully exert brawn causes the Guardian to lose centeredness and the ability to quickly adapt to changing situations. The overly brawny Guardian often resorts to courage rather than intelligence, thus taking unnecessary risks, which imperil both him and the Mission. This may seem to be quite an extrapolation on a simple nutcracking exercise, yet it is a potent illustration of how training is life. The way we crack nuts is the way we function on a Mission. We can't help but do so, as we are creatures of habit. Because of this, we take this and all other training exercises seriously.

An Elite Exercise: Switch Training

Have you ever felt out of place and taken on another persona in order to fit in? Were you ever about to get caught red-handed at doing something, and you saved yourself by making it appear as though you were doing something else? How often have you wondered about that innocent look on your kids' faces when you walked into their room and suspected they were up to some mischief?

We've all seen it and we've all done it because it is an innate skill that we each possess. Like Chameleons who can change color to blend into a fluctuating background, we can quickly change our posture, facial expressions, focus, and tone of voice. We do this to create the illusion that we are completely involved in something other than what actually has—or just had—our attention. We want to draw someone's attention away from where our attention was a mere second ago.

We Humans evolved this ability back when we lived as hunter-gatherers. In order to stalk an animal successfully, we had to learn how to approach her nonchalantly. Rather than focusing on her and approaching directly—which would spook her—we would act as though we didn't notice her and were just passing through, maybe picking berries.

Switch Training uses this inborn attention-shifting skill, only with other people instead of on a hunt. The goal of the Training is to be fully engaged in an exercise without the people around us having the slightest clue as to what we are doing. It is the epitome of being like a shadow—and it is one of the most difficult forms of training, for these reasons:

- **We need to stay present and aware** with both the exercise and those who are (or might be) observing us.

- **We have to maintain our level of training**, without it looking like we are training.

- **We are developing two skill sets simultaneously**: the primary exercise skill and stealth.

▓ **We need to learn to practice the skill without being hurtfully deceptive.**

Switch Training works with any exercise that can potentially be disguised. Yet no matter what the exercise, Switch Training makes the exercise several times more demanding than it normally is. For this reason, *do not attempt Switch Training with an exercise until you have become proficient at that exercise.* Time and again I have seen people attempt Switch Training before they are ready, and it leads to frustration and failure.

A special frame of mind is needed in order for Switch Training to work.

First: Develop the following five mindsets until they become second Nature to you:

1. **Go into an exercise cold.** This means *have no expectations* and *do not psych yourself up*. Be fully present and fully engaged in every movement.

2. **Know how to listen.** This takes getting out of your ego and realizing that you are hearing, seeing, and feeling not for you, but for the Mission.

3. **Improvise.** Every movement gets fine-tuned, adjusting to the ever-changing now.

4. **There is no failure.** As soon as we think so, we negate the first three mindsets, get locked in the past, and start future projecting.

5. **Accept full responsibility—and blame if need be.** I am the pack, I am the Mission, and my actions extend far beyond myself.

Second: Review these mindsets immediately before an exercise, so they are at the forefront of your consciousness.

Here is a traditional Zen story that shows Switch Training in action:

In a remote district lived a Sage and a group of Seekers who had dedicated themselves to the study and understanding of the Ancient Teachings.

"We are coming to resemble Scholars," announced the Sage one day. "Let us burn every note and book and abandon every practice that we have accumulated."

"How enlightened!" commented the Seekers. "By releasing ourselves of our conventions and accoutrements, we will arrive at the Essence!"

Not long after, the governor issued a ban on all scholarly studies and exercises. All books on Ancient Wisdom were to be burned, and any practitioners would be severely punished.

Many of the people took up the cause. Gangs scoured neighborhoods, focusing on houses where they suspected contraband.

When a gang came to the cabin of the Sage and the Seekers, they found everyone out in the yard, having a good time burning texts. After some shared reverie, the gang took off, with the two groups cheering each other on.

The story demonstrates Switch Training at its finest: two groups engaged in the same activity and appearing to be in complete harmony with each other, yet under the surface they are acting for entirely different reasons. Here is stealth in the guise of naked exposure and camaraderie where there could easily have been confrontation.

Imagine the consequences if the timing was off, or if any of the Seekers panicked under the pressure. To be able to dance in the face of potential disaster requires a level of training that humbles me every time I dare think I have achieved it.

Chapter 18 Citations

1   "Telling Warrior Stories with Hula" https://www.youtube.com/watch?v=BFT-M18N2A4 (accessed June 20, 2020)

2   Bob Dylan, "Subterranean Homesick Blues," *Bob Dylan*, http://www.bobdylan.com/songs/subterranean-homesick-blues/ (accessed October 12, 2019).

CHAPTER 19

DAILY REFLECTIONS

Serving our people and protecting our Mother is more than a calling. It is a way of life that permeates our being. No matter what we think or do—and whether or not we are aware of it in any moment—we are living and breathing the Guardian Way.

Like an obsession that is never completely satisfied, we can't get away from it. At any time of day or night, the rumbling from deep within could surface. It might be triggered by a political injustice, a child without guidance, or a grove of elder trees being sacrificed to greed. It could come from some unknown source. Whatever the case, it must be answered, or it plagues us like a lost and starving puppy.

To answer the calling, we first need to hear it clearly, then determine the direction from which it comes. But we are often busy. Our minds are cluttered. We are stressed. So we tune out the calling or we brush it aside.

There is a way to fine-tune our consciousness to the Guardian frequency. It's the first thing I do every morning when I wake up, and I return to it periodically throughout the day. Some people call it a daily reflection, meditation, or mantra. For me, it's just an echo of what's already in my heart—a reminder of who I am and what really matters in life. I'd like to share this practice with you to see if it might help you as it has helped me.

The following is a morsel of Guardian Consciousness for every day of the year. Together, they portray the heart and soul of the Guardian Way. Use them any way that speaks to you:

separately as daily meditations, either randomly or by date, or together as an inspirational reading.

Jan. 1: Gather all needed information before beginning to plan.

Jan. 2: Approach large Missions methodically.

Jan. 3: Make all preparations well in advance.

Jan. 4: Whatever is possible is limited by what I can see.

Jan. 5: Without full presence and consistent follow-through, expect to fail.

Jan. 6: My goal is fully achievable only when it becomes the process.

Jan. 7: Be the nimble cat when training and the steady bear when on a Mission.

Jan. 8: Respond immediately when it becomes clear that there needs to be a change of plan.

Jan. 9: Don't do anything just because it makes sense.

Jan. 10: Honor Elders not only in word, but by incorporating their essence into my life and sharing.

Jan. 11: Answers lie not ahead, but in returning to the source.

Jan. 12: Progress deliberately and systematically.

Jan. 13: Plan a Mission only on what is solidly present and available.

Jan. 14: Eliminate everything extraneous and I'll eliminate most potential trip-ups.

Jan. 15: Engagement is what makes things work.

Jan. 16: On a Mission, allow no distractions and proceed at the greatest speed that does not compromise integrity.

Jan. 17: A margin of safety is gained when I realize that everything is more than—and other than—it appears.

Jan. 18: On a Mission, always keep the goal in mind.

Jan. 19: When not being stealthy, be blatant.

Jan. 20: Perspective before action.

Jan. 21: Perform at around two-thirds capacity, so that I'll have reserve to draw upon if necessary.

Jan. 22: Working together encourages harmony; working separately sets the stage for conflict.

Jan. 23: A small error in judgment carries a big risk.

Jan. 24: Dilemmas are solved by listening.

Jan. 25: A Mission is best accomplished by making each step its own goal.

Jan. 26: Perspective cannot be gained without considering context. Then, once perspective is gained, get specific.

Jan. 27: Be diligent with each and every piece of the Mission puzzle.

Jan. 28: Avoid plans that limit results.

Jan. 29: Blend approaches and I will expand possibilities.

Jan. 30: In awkward situations, first get centered, then respond.

Jan. 31: When there is a challenge, there is a way to surmount it.

Feb. 1: Be clear, consistent, inclusive, and solid with follow-through.

Feb. 2: On a Mission, utilize what is available rather than trying to create something new.

Feb. 3: Unfamiliarity creates fear. Embrace fear and unfamiliarity becomes a curiosity, which leads to familiarity.

Feb. 4: Continually fine-tune what I am doing.

Feb. 5: Be careful of getting ahead of myself.

Feb. 6: Making choices is playing the odds.

Feb. 7: Stress stifles adaptability.

Feb. 8: What is most practical is not always what best meets my people's needs.

Feb. 9: Ignore convention and find the best way.

Feb. 10: New options present themselves when I switch from my head to my heart.

Feb. 11: Rather than just getting something done, give attention to the quality of my work.

Feb. 12: Give time for integrating something new.

Feb. 13: There is no goal, only the journey.

Feb. 14: The only errors are in judgment.

Feb. 15: Follow-through is everything.

Feb. 16: Keep informed.

Feb. 17: Expectations interfere with flow.

Feb. 18: When I feel out of place, immediately create an aura of comfort.

Feb. 19: Be thorough, yet concise, with all descriptions.

Feb. 20: A sense of wonder opens me to the realm of possibilities.

Feb. 21: The Path to anywhere is one of constant negotiation.

Feb. 22: When training out on my edge, expect the joy of discovery and the sadness of losing the familiar.

Feb. 23: Progress should be steady, unrushed, and based on a solid plan.

Feb. 24: Tend to potential disruptions preemptively, taking care not to overreact.

Feb. 25: When something isn't working, turn to what worked in the past before attempting something new.

Feb. 26: Do not progress without being fully prepared.

Feb. 27: Clutter breeds confusion. Simplify, simplify, simplify.

Feb. 28: The faster I go, the more I miss and the harder progress becomes.

Feb. 29: When I feel frustrated, it's because I've chosen that as an option.

Mar. 1: Discomfort ought not be a determining factor.

Mar. 2: On a newly trodden Path, expect the unexpected.

Mar. 3: Imposing my will creates resistance to progress. Whenever possible, align with what is.

Mar. 4: I will not be overwhelmed when I am fully present and integrated.

Mar. 5: The practice needs to be more demanding than the application.

Mar. 6: Engage in hostility only as a last resort.

Mar. 7: Safeguard the well-being of others by assuring a low level of stress and a high level of personal satisfaction.

Mar. 8: Defend those who are being persecuted or falsely accused.

Mar. 9: Stand up for the exploited and disadvantaged.

Mar. 10: Protect others from their own follies, shortsightedness, and errors of judgment.

Mar. 11: Grant the utmost respect and space to those who attempt to thwart our Mission.

Mar. 12: When I have no choice but to fight, do not pit myself against anything, but rather battle for Balance.

Mar. 13: The aim of training is not to be bigger, stronger, faster, or braver, but rather to be successful in serving my people.

Mar. 14: Empowering skills do not inflate the ego; they bring it rest.

Mar. 15: Function from my Heart-of-Hearts and my emotions will serve rather than control me.

Mar. 16: When I find myself overwhelmed by emotion, withdraw and re-center myself in my Heart-of-Hearts.

Mar. 17: Training is never complete—it continues without respite. Life is training, and training is life.

Mar. 18: Regularly find ways to express gratitude.

Mar. 19: When there is no present challenge, create one.

Mar. 20: To become Balanced, dive into Chaos.

Mar. 21: Shun security and remain alert.

Mar. 22: Engage in something as though it is my last opportunity to do so.

Mar. 23: Everything I experience is ultimately for service.

Mar. 24: There are two approaches to conflict: the blame-shame game, or deep listening and empathy.

Mar. 25: Play to lose—but just barely lose.

Mar. 26: The greater satisfaction comes from knowing my abilities without needing to prove them.

Mar. 27: Step into the unknown—I know I have no other choice.

Mar. 28: Dance on the edge of what I think is possible.

Mar. 29: Do not talk anyone into anything. Rather, serve those who are ready.

Mar. 30: Scout ahead, yet keep an eye on the flanks and rear.

Mar. 31: The needs of the pack are my needs—meet its needs first.

Apr. 1: Prepare for all possible scenarios.

Apr. 2: What matters most is the safety of children and Elders.

Apr. 3: To solve nagging problems, find what others have missed.

Apr. 4: With anything new, first listen and observe.

Apr. 5: Represent my people honorably and wisely.

Apr. 6: Always act as though I am a guest.

Apr. 7: Always scout ahead, even in familiar territory.

Apr. 8: Learn to move undetected.

Apr. 9: Camouflage is only a screen. Learn instead to become invisible.

Apr. 10: Move only within the greater movement.

Apr. 11: Develop my innate skills without bending them to outside influence.

Apr. 12: Strengthen my relationships—they are the foundation of my support and ability to serve.

Apr. 13: Serve dispassionately.

Apr. 14: Provide for myself last and least.

Apr. 15: All Missions are stealth Missions.

Apr. 16: Develop communication skills before and above all others.

Apr. 17: Eat the foods that support optimum Guardian performance.

Apr. 18: Fast one day a week, and three days every couple months.

Apr. 19: Be the last one to exit. Eat the scraps, leftovers, and pan scrapings.

Apr. 20: When there are parcels to carry, take the heaviest or most awkward ones.

Apr. 21: Take the least comfortable seat, and hold doors for those less able than me.

Apr. 22: Take perimeter positions in groups, and stay attuned to the surroundings.

Apr. 23: Options don't preexist; they are created by exploration.

Apr. 24: Create openings for others to develop and display their talents.

Apr. 25: Provide training opportunities for younger Guardians.

Apr. 26: Base my life on the principle that giving is receiving.

Apr. 27: Become as free-flowing as water in a stream, ready to twist with the bends, ride the riffles, and split to go around rocks.

Apr. 28: Pick up and clean up anything that despoils the Mother's countenance.

Apr. 29: Be a nonentity: as anonymous, detached, and pliable as a shadow.

Apr. 30: Be the antithesis of courageous: Be calculated and seemingly disconnected.

May 1: Approach a Mission like breathing: with no thought about success or failure, or what it might bring.

May 2: Practice maintaining sensory perspective without focusing on any particular sight or sound.

May 3: Let feelings flow through like the breeze in the treetops.

May 4: Align with the energies at play, without preference or prejudice.

May 5: Do as much as I can by not doing.

May 6: Use my mind to join rather than divide.

May 7: Whenever the enemy mindset surfaces, either re-center in dispassion or disengage.

May 8: Realize that there is a belief attached to everything I see, do, and say.

May 9: Learn to toss a belief aside as quickly and easily as a wrong-sized wrench.

May 10: Be a walking contradiction, ever-changing with the changes around me.

May 11: Accidents, failures, and mistakes are eye-openers, teachers, and opportunities.

May 12: Admit that I am a fool.

May 13: Fail often.

May 14: Never try; only do.

May 15: Choices arise from lack of clarity and direction.

May 16: With constant fine-tuning, there is no need for trial and error.

May 17: Build trust on presence and knowledge rather than faith and projections.

May 18: Changing my patterns is the only way I can change myself.

May 19: Make no assumptions, and take nothing for granted.

May 20: Treat no two things alike.

May 21: Learn by listening to the stories of my fellow Guardians.

May 22: Dedicate myself to continual transformation.

May 23: Be ever unpredictable and spontaneous.

May 24: Refrain from doing the same thing in the same way twice in a row.

May 25: Engage consciously in whatever is before me.

May 26: Always observing, always serving.

May 27: Everything I do matters, as it affects not only the present, but the past and future as well.

May 28: The only way to fully know the moment is to become it.

May 29: Become the person who is speaking.

May 30: Treat training as un-training.

May 31: Dwell in an arena of dynamic tension without being in a state of dynamic tension.

June 1: Forget exercise and think movement.

June 2: Make training a natural component of daily living.

June 3: Stretch my muscles whenever I feel the urge.

June 4: Exercise aerobically every other day for twenty to thirty minutes.

June 5: Live limber to stay limber.

June 6: Avoid repetitive-motion training.

June 7: Unlearn rather than learn.

June 8: Practice running shirtless, and on unprepared surfaces.

June 9: Practice free-form dance as a training exercise.

June 10: Learn how to maintain centeredness in shameful situations.

June 11: Immediately upon waking, keep my eyes closed and attune to the surrounding environment.

June 12: In relationships, seek complementarity over compatibility.

June 13: Don't think, wish, or dream, but do!

June 14: On a Mission, take no chances and play no odds.

June 15: Realize that the only constant is change.

June 16: Wear noiseless clothing and minimalist, form-fitting footwear.

June 17: Always carry a small, all-purpose knife.

June 18: Do not carry emotional baggage into a Mission.

June 19: Be as a question.

June 20: Make no assumptions and take nothing for granted.

June 21: If performance anxiety hits, deconstruct the Mission into small steps.

June 22: When I look for a lush meadow and find only barren ground, it's a perfect place to sit and listen.

June 23: Don't rely on luck.

June 24: Keep gear minimal and comprised of multifunctional items.

June 25: Turn first to what is in-hand or immediately available.

June 26: Approach Missions as though they were hunts, which in essence they are.

June 27: For the Guardian, confidence is a dirty word.

June 28: Cultivate comfort by being uncomfortable.

June 29: When I am tracking, my only ethical consideration is to become one with my quarry.

June 30: Be precise and brief with all pack and Mission-related communication.

July 1: When anxious or stressed, immediately relax my jaw, then breathe deeply and slowly.

July 2: I carry no weapons; instead, I train my mind. I will be safer and can then more easily defeat someone with a weapon.

July 3: Win by not winning, and by creating no losers.

July 4: Bluff only if I can back it up if my bluff is called.

July 5: Have more than one sure escape route.

July 6: Train for physical confrontation by learning to listen.

July 7: Develop the creativity and ingenuity to accommodate—and take me beyond—my limitations.

July 8: Doing something for a future goal is not doing it.

July 9: Keep training as unstructured and playful as possible.

July 10: Specialization can be crippling.

July 11: Always underschedule.

July 12: Train not because it's good for me, but because I love it.

July 13: No one is the best at anything.

July 14: There is no reality; there is only the picture I create by my perceptions and beliefs.

July 15: Train to see what happens before it happens.

July 16: I get some of my best training in my dreams.

July 17: Before launching a Mission, visualize its completion.

July 18: Give 100 percent and I live 100 percent.

July 19: Act like the Mission is a life-or-death matter.

July 20: In a confrontation, cater to my opponent's ego rather than aggravating it.

July 21: Someone who is challenged hears either "You are wrong" or "You're a liar."

July 22: I become what I fight.

July 23: Protect others from harm in a way that won't bring more harm.

July 24: My worst enemy is myself.

July 25: Fully own my life and my feelings.

July 26: Be accountable for my choices *and* their ripple effects.

July 27: Do not be flashy when performing on a Mission.

July 28: Embrace fear when it arises, and it becomes my guide rather than my oppressor.

July 29: Awareness is the first and most necessary step to mastery.

July 30: Be thankful when things fall apart.

July 31: The less I talk, the more I can hear what my people need.

Aug. 1: Whenever possible, signaling should be two-way, to confirm reception and reduce the chance of misinterpretation.

Aug. 2: When a Mission is in jeopardy, instantly meld into the shadows.

Aug. 3: Trust not only in what I can do now, but in what I've learned over my entire life.

Aug. 4: Breathe through my nose as much as possible, even when running.

Aug. 5: Use a checklist to become more productive. Make no more than seven or eight entries.

Aug. 6: Engage in every action with honor and respect; make every utterance a prayer of gratitude.

Aug. 7: Value imagination over knowledge.

Aug. 8: Make my bed first thing every morning.

Aug. 9: Expect fairness and I cloud my vision.

Aug. 10: Assume people are going to stay the way they are.

Aug. 11: Shun mediocrity.

Aug. 12: Embrace relevant facts, no matter what their source.

Aug. 13: Align action with purpose.

Aug. 14: Walk in the footsteps of those I wish to emulate.

Aug. 15: Seek first to understand, then to be understood.

Aug. 16: Always look at more than one alternative. Strength comes from diversity.

Aug. 17: There is no way to be right.

Aug. 18: Every outcome is the right outcome.

Aug. 19: The obstacle is the way.

Aug. 20: There are only setbacks when I quit learning.

Aug. 21: Gain energy by expending the energy I have.

Aug. 22: Build new habits instead of trying to break old ones.

Aug. 23: Surround myself with those I want to resemble, and it will happen.

Aug. 24: To enrich life and improve performance, I continually train my senses.

Aug. 25: Embrace ambiguity, paradox, and uncertainty, as they are more real than clarity, regularity, and sureness.

Aug. 26: Negative and positive perceptions undermine centeredness and mask clarity.

Aug. 27: Embrace pain in all its forms, for it spurs action.

Aug. 28: Never know who I am; be ever the Seeker-Trainee.

Aug. 29: Differences of opinion and perspective are signs of a well-functioning pack.

Aug. 30: Hidden in a person's deepest feelings is her true story.

Aug. 31: When working with forces greater than myself, treat them with ultimate respect and stay out of harm's way.

Sept. 1: The present reveals itself through stories of the past.

Sept. 2: Hold off on all decisions until it is absolutely necessary to make them; and even then keep thoroughly exploring all options.

Sept. 3: The richness lies in the experience of discovering, rather than in the discovery itself.

Sept. 4: When I hear "no," it means "Keep working to find a way."

Sept. 5: Take what is available and transform it into what is needed.

Sept. 6: Move on responsibly and in a timely manner.

Sept. 7: Stealth requires that every thought and move be impeccable.

Sept. 8: The cost of denial is too high to pay.

Sept. 9: Be a catalyst.

Sept. 10: When a plan fails, stick with the plan.

Sept. 11: Beneath pain and suffering lie pearls of awareness.

Sept. 12: The smallest details deserve attention.

Sept. 13: Hunger is best satiated slowly.

Sept. 14: Even if I have a solution, keep considering alternatives.

Sept. 15: An extreme emotional response can lead to a breakthrough.

Sept. 16: Meet needs in a gentle, supportive, nurturing way.

Sept. 17: Find the joy in whatever I do.

Sept. 18: Drop conviction and embrace perspective.

Sept. 19: Keep pace with my packmates, and help them keep pace with me.

Sept. 20: Look at my secondary reasons for doing things.

Sept. 21: Find the solution in the situation.

Sept. 22: Soothe an irreconcilable difference by creating an unrelated but overriding resonance.

Sept. 23: Approach everything with the same dedication and passion.

Sept. 24: Listen and speak gently, as gentleness is a greater force than anger or any other emotional charge.

Sept. 25: There is nowhere to hide.

Sept. 26: Stealth in training, stealth in being.

Sept. 27: A Mission is formulated by its intention, rather than by the Guardians involved.

Sept. 28: Attention to detail brings results.

Sept. 29: The first two steps in planning a Mission: Clarify it, then strip it down to its essence.

Sept. 30: Base actions on present rather than past circumstances.

Oct. 1: The Path less traveled brings my people undiscovered riches.

Oct. 2: Drop the story that divides.

Oct. 3: Address conflict immediately.

Oct. 4: Become fully present and engaged before proceeding.

Oct. 5: When there is resistance, look for the reason before trying to overcome it.

Oct. 6: Give time for integrating something new.

Oct. 7: When looking for a replacement, find something as close as possible to the original.

Oct. 8: An emotionally charged issue takes a structured, safe, and gingerly approach.

Oct. 9: Large-scale change creates large-scale issues. Address these by breaking them down into small, clear segments.

Oct. 10: Treat stressful situations as though they were Guardian Missions.

Oct. 11: First take care of the small stuff; this gives undivided time and energy for the big stuff.

Oct. 12: Reach people where they are.

Oct. 13: Presence solves long- and short-term issues.

Oct. 14: Avoid assumptions, as they are based on a past that can get shy about repeating itself.

Oct. 15: There are always other ways.

Oct. 16: Use other people's ideas rather than mine whenever they make a comparable contribution.

Oct. 17: My ability to change is my ability to give.

Oct. 18: When receiving criticism, first listen, then acknowledge what was spoken, then express gratitude for it.

Oct. 19: From the amorphous mass, I either tease forth nurturance or cause it to shy away.

Oct. 20: As independently as possible, use what is right at my disposal to meet my immediate needs.

Oct. 21: My goal is real when I experience it in every step I take toward it.

Oct. 22: The Way of the Guardian is an approach to life rather than a practice.

Oct. 23: Gain outside perspective before acting. When there is nothing to go on, borrow from a parallel situation.

Oct. 24: My talents are needed. I am making them available.

Oct. 25: Working together encourages harmony; working separately sets the stage for conflict.

Oct. 26: Confusion and disconnectedness result from my inability to adapt to a situation.

Oct. 27: There is no need to immediately understand the unexpected. Just embrace it.

Oct. 28: Be most generous with those who are absent.

Oct. 29: When I arrive, I am only halfway there.

Oct. 30: Borrowing from the past can greatly facilitate moving forward.

Oct. 31: Take care of the periphery, and find the missing piece.

Nov. 1: Persist, yet with sensitivity and presence.

Nov. 2: My forgetfulness is a voice asking me why I am not engaged enough to remember.

Nov. 3: Consider the total effect of my intent before acting.

Nov. 4: Every direction I choose is tainted with my subjective sight.

Nov. 5: The more stripped-down the approach, the more effective it can be.

Nov. 6: No matter what I take on, it's going to take time, energy, and space.

Nov. 7: An imminent victory can blind me to its intrinsic tragedy.

Nov. 8: The core of a Guardian Mission is making connections.

Nov. 9: Expect unexpected challenges with anything new.

Nov. 10: Only by dancing out on my edge will I discover the full range of my talents and abilities.

Nov. 11: When I get caught in a trap, turn around and walk out.

Nov. 12: Change takes dedicated energy. At the same time, be wary of fatigue.

Nov. 13: I take full blame for anything in which I am involved.

Nov. 14: I need to be in the mire to best see what could be of help in getting out of it.

Nov. 15: Make every step go smoothly, for each step is a goal. The ultimate goal will then spontaneously manifest.

Nov. 16: Proceed only with quality time and materials.

Nov. 17: At mid-Mission, reconnoiter and reassess.

Nov. 18: The Guardian dwells under the guise of the ordinary.

Nov. 19: My continual Mission is to seek alignment.

Nov. 20: Every movement and observation is walking into a question.

Nov. 21: Continually start over, to keep bringing in fresh perspective.

Nov. 22: Above all, provide comfort and security.

Nov. 23: Venture out on my edge, get trashed, and bring home the treasure.

Nov. 24: Be careful going forward, lest I have to backtrack.

Nov. 25: So much of what I do is to provide nurturance and support for my centeredness.

Nov. 26: By doing each step well, I come to better understand the goal.

Nov. 27: When I settle for working with what I have, it's time for change.

Nov. 28: A need begs immediate follow-through.

Nov. 29: Support can come from where I least expect it.

Nov. 30: A Mission debriefing is an opportunity to step back, listen afresh, incorporate new voices, and seek out the next Mission.

Dec. 1: Whatever I do when I feel uncentered is going to be uncentered.

Dec. 2: Address a topic clearly enough so that people don't have to keep asking questions.

Dec. 3: Life is spontaneous training.

Dec. 4: What matters as much as the quality of what I offer is how it can be shared.

Dec. 5: Giving disproportionate attention to or avoiding any individual hurts the pack.

Dec. 6: Make sure I'm following my heart rather than the desires of others.

Dec. 7: There is always more than one reason.

Dec. 8: Contribute what I can to the moment's situation, then move on.

Dec. 9: To draw in people, an involvement needs to be engaging and uncomplicated.

Dec. 10: Effective change is lived rather than preached.

Dec. 11: Doubt and continuous challenge tell me I'm on the right path.

Dec. 12: When I see what others don't, I need to share it.

Dec. 13: When I use force of will to accomplish something, I become enslaved to my will.

Dec. 14: Develop my capacities not because I need them, but just because they exist.

Dec. 15: Working together encourages harmony; working separately sets the stage for conflict.

Dec. 16: More of the same begets only more of the same.

Dec. 17: When assembling or organizing something, inspect each component thoroughly.

Dec. 18: Find maturity in a relationship the moment it begins.

Dec. 19: Approach everything with the same dedication and dis-passion.

Dec. 20: Every component is as valued and sacred as the whole.

Dec. 21: Choose the best option. Then revisit the others to see what can be gained from them.

Dec. 22: When I think I can't meet my own expectations, it's time to think creatively.

Dec. 23: Further develop the subtle and sensitive aspects of my approach.

Dec. 24: Listen with acuteness and sensitivity, then make a deci-sion and give it all I've got.

Dec. 25: The more unclear my direction, the more risk I take in traveling.

Dec. 26: Completely immerse myself in a situation—and look beneath it—before forming any opinions about it.

Dec. 27: The only good ideas are those that can be successfully applied.

Dec. 28: Find points of resonance to open doors, rather than forcing them open.

Dec. 29: A patchwork approach creates confusion and compro-mised results.

Dec. 30: When results fall short of effort, take a break, breathe, then take another tack.

Dec. 31: Be wary of rationalizing to justify an action.

PART IV

THE MISSION

A Guardian's full attention is devoted to the ever-changing now, and his only concern is the smooth, flawless functioning of his pack. The pack is his being and the Mission is his world.

In this section, we enter the world of the Mission. Here everything comes together that you have learned thus far. You immerse yourself in the experience of running with a dedicated and highly accomplished band of comrades. After setting up a camp in a strategic outback location, you plan and execute a vital Mission. Moving as invisibly as a shadow in the shadows, you signal to your packmates in ways that look like nothing more than a branch swaying slightly in the breeze.

Yet you are detected—someone jumps in front of you with a gun. You are purposefully unarmed because you know you are safer to be so in a situation like this than if you too had a weapon. Yet you have something far more powerful and disarming. Drawing from your Training, you not only pacify her, but you bring her around to your side with nothing more than the power of your mind.

Welcome to the climax of your Training.

INTO THE CONSCIOUSNESS

It's dawn on a secluded bog island in a remote wilderness. The pack taking my Guardian Intensive Training is heading out from their *Stealth Camp* on the island for a Mission to clean up a toxic waste site in a restricted area. As they silently cross the bog to reach the highland, one of the Trainees whispers to the next, "It's the middle of July—what are we doing breaking through ice?"

They're barefoot, and with every step they crack the thin skin of ice and sink into cold water and muck up to their knees. Even though it's unseasonably cold, they don't feel it. With their synchronous movement and sense of purpose, they have transcended discomfort and become the Mission. The pack has entered Guardian Consciousness.

How It Works

Our mind is comprised of three brains: reptilian, mammalian, and primate. The reptilian governs our basic survival and reproductive needs; the primate is our rational-linear processor; and the mammalian (or *limbic process*) is the seat of long-term memories, emotion, and empathy. As previously mentioned, 95 to 99 percent of our mental functioning occurs subconsciously in the limbic process. When Guardians come together in a state of Guardian Consciousness, they function in *limbic resonance.* It is in this limbic-brain consciousness that we are most functional and have the greatest access to our capabilities. And it is in limbic consciousness that we step beyond our egos and become capable of functioning as an organ within an organism.

As an organism, I don't have a choice in which heart or legs or face I'm given. I need to embrace my whole being and allow my parts to work together synchronously. The same is true with my pack: All members do the best with what they are given and pull together as one organism for the success of the Mission.

The Role of Peer Influence

Another contributor to Guardian Consciousness is the role our packmates play. For social beings such as us, it is important that our peers impact us. In fact, we could not survive long without it, as we would soon be thrust apart in a swirl of ego-driven conflicts.

We thrive on *peer influence* because it helps us:

- Find meaning, motivation, and inspiration
- Recognize what we are blind to
- Receive relevant guidance
- Do our best in service to our people
- Embrace a shared vision

It is for all five of these reasons that a conscious and well-developed sense of peer influence is vital to the functioning of a Guardian pack. Peer influence helps us to become one voice, one spirit, and one purpose, or we are not a pack by any definition.

When peer influence becomes ego driven, it morphs into *peer pressure*. While peer influence supports personal empowerment and the Circle Way, peer pressure is socially divisive and personally repressive.

Peer pressure can cause chronic stress or emotional scarring, which may result in inferiority complexes and depression.

In extreme cases, some people become traumatized. Bullying is one of the more insidious forms of peer pressure.

Peer influence helps us develop and sustain Guardian Consciousness. Anyone who struggles to be in resonance with the pack is given immediate attention. In the evolution of a pack, peer influence is perhaps the most potent and effective healing tool. By quickly bringing dysfunctional relational patterns to the surface and focusing healing attention upon them, peer influence helps us break through the maladaptive behavioral patterns that sometimes get in the way.

A Puzzling Way to Build Consciousness

Above all, a successful Guardian Mission requires a pack whose members function together as seamlessly as the organs in a body. This flow state requires:

- Complete relaxation of the ego
- A shared vision of the Guardian Way
- The skills to become and function in a pack

Notice I didn't say "the skills to execute a Mission." Those are secondary and come much easier—and are far more useful—when we become the pack and together lose ourselves in the Mission, rather than seeing ourselves as individual performers. This is true of any team that is not a one-win wonder, but can sustain its quality performance over time and produce consistent and reliable results.

For this Pack Consciousness training exercise, we need three things:

- **A 1,000-piece jigsaw picture puzzle** with a medium to high degree of difficulty
- **Three to five people**
- **Three hours** of uninterrupted time

I specially select puzzles for my Trainees, to assure that they receive the best possible training tools. Just as Guardians step forward to serve on whatever Mission is presented to better the lot of their people, Trainees willingly accept whatever puzzle is given or sent to them.

Their Training History

The first jigsaw puzzles, called dissected maps, were developed in London to help children learn geography.[1] Over the years, puzzles have taken an increasingly more prominent role in childhood development. They contribute to problem-solving skills and manual dexterity, and they provide a sense of accomplishment. For older adults, puzzles help maintain mental acuity.

This exercise serves as a metaphor for all Missions. Putting a puzzle together is no different than putting a Mission together. We employ the same four-step process with both:

1. Start out with a bunch of seemingly unrelated components.
2. Pull them together into a cohesive unit.
3. Grasp the full picture.
4. Become the Mission.

During this exercise, the individual puzzle pieces seem to disappear as they merge into the picture, just as individual pack members disappear as they merge into the Mission. This is one of the easiest and most effective exercises for developing pack functioning skills. It can be done nearly anywhere and its requirements are easily met. The results are clear and immediate, which makes them easy to evaluate and apply to real-world situations.

Before You Begin

Without looking, reach in the box, grab several puzzle pieces, and set them aside. No Mission picture is ever complete, either when envisioning the Mission or when it is concluded.

The Four Puzzle Training Skills

Following are the essential functioning abilities this exercise helps us develop. With each one, start slowly and consciously, so that you are fully present and engaged in the moment. Speed, which is often an important component in a Guardian Mission, gradually and naturally picks up as you become more and more adept with these skills.

1. Listening

Speed and efficiency in assembling a puzzle has everything to do with picking up on the verbal and nonverbal cues from our pack members:

* Who is assembling the frame?
* Who is focusing on which quadrants of the puzzle?
* Who is good at matching colors?
* Who is good at matching forms and shapes?
* Who has pieces organized in groupings?

These are the various organs performing their individual functions in the organism. Becoming aware of these functions within this consciousness makes the difference between a free-for-all, with individuals randomly assembling a puzzle with no communication, and a coordinated effort. While the first approach can take ten or more hours to finish the puzzle, the same group can complete the puzzle in around three hours—if they simply listen to each other.

The core difference between the two approaches is that the first is ego-centered, and the second is immersion-centered. With the second strategy, the ego-centered individual disappears. All of an individual's talents and skills are thus devoted to the process. This immersion is what makes the seamless pack approach the task much more efficiently.

Oh, and I should mention: After you decide who is performing which tasks, you assemble the puzzle silently, just as though you were on a Mission. And there is no looking at the picture on the box cover.

2. Respect

With several people working together so closely, both in physical and mental proximity, it is essential that they respect one another's space. Like the organs in a body, each individual needs a certain amount of autonomy in order to function to her fullest. Sometimes the excitement of the chase takes over: You find a puzzle piece that you know fits right under the hand of the person next to you. But if you were to push her aside to put the piece in place, it would interrupt her flow and create a win-lose situation. This is not a good way to complete the Mission as quickly and efficiently as possible. Instead of crowding her out, you could follow another lead, knowing that you can go back and pop in that sure piece when there is an opening.

When everyone adopts this give-and-take approach, a synchronicity begins to evolve that makes the assembly of the puzzle seem as though it is choreographed. If you filmed a well-attuned pack from above and viewed it at fast speed, you would see each individual moving seamlessly within the greater movement, with respect continually shown by how they respond to and feed off of each other. To me, it resembles a well-choreographed dance.

3. Participation

Here is where we go from theory to practice and start functioning as one organism. There is no ego present, and the group's needs replace the needs of each individual. The bliss is in being. It comes from immersion in the moment and nothing else. We are consumed with a sense of *doing* rather than *accomplishing*. When we feel an overriding sense of belonging, of relationship, we have created the desired synergy that defines

Mission Consciousness. We have become the interaction—we then *are* the puzzle pieces bringing themselves together. We are following a greater calling for wholeness, for completion.

4. Execution

It's all about complementarity, which goes beyond compatibility. It's not good enough to just get along while we are working together—we need to mesh with each other, just as the puzzle pieces do. When they come together, they cease to exist as individual entities. A puzzle piece is only a part of some meaningless past: a random squiggle on an oddly shaped piece of paperboard, useless and irrelevant to anything beyond itself. Like your heart or your liver outside your body, the piece has no function, no reason for being, and no way to sustain itself. It is only in the execution of the roles for which they are designed that the heart and liver find their senses of purpose and fulfillment. The same is true of the Guardian. Only actions speak, and it is in the doing—and *how* it is done—that the Guardian justifies not only his existence but the existence of his people.

The next time you see a puzzle, recognize it for what it is: the ultimate training tool. The table on which you lay the pieces is your Mission site. Send out the howl to call your pack together, and let the Training begin!

Intuition Training

Sharpening our intuitive skills is a good complement to Puzzle Training. The Secret Stone Game *is an effective intuitive trainer that I learned from indigenous peoples. You'll find it referenced in Chapter 2 under* Skill Level.

What Undermines Mission Consciousness

The pack is our being and the Mission is our world. Yet there are times when contrary energies come into play. Following are the four that are most commonly encountered.

1. Playing the Odds

An important and often-overlooked element of Mission Consciousness is *chance*. Our rational mind constantly plays the odds: Am I going to make it to work on time? Will I have enough money to go skiing this weekend? What are the chances that this person will go out on a date with me?

This continuous rational questioning creates a dilemma on the Mission, when there is no room for odds-playing. There must be as much certainty as possible, providing a solid underpinning for the ever-changing now. Odds-playing can detract from Mission success for these reasons:

- Odds cannot be relied upon.
- Playing the odds clouds Mission focus.
- Odds do not improve over time.

The rational mind incorrectly assumes that odds improve over time. If I keep asking people out for dates and keep getting refused, I think that if I persist, my chances will improve and eventually someone will agree to go out with me. Many gamblers rationalize that the longer their losing streak, the closer they come to winning.

However, this is nothing more than a trick of the mind. If I lose a hundred times in a row, my odds of winning are exactly the same the next time as they were the very first time. This apparent glitch in our rational process is a boon for the card shark and gambling casino; however, it is the bane of a Mission. This is one reason that *Don't think—do!* is a Mission motto. Thinking has to happen before, not during a Mission. All we do during a Mission is adapt and adjust.

Why does the rational mind play tricks on us such as odds-playing? It is the mind's sly way of keeping us motivated, which is necessary in survival situations such as the ones in which our species evolved. If we didn't believe our odds on the hunt would improve after repeated failed attempts, we might quit and our people would starve.

The only way to improve our odds is to incorporate what we learn from our failures. However, there is no way to improve the toss of the dice or the dealing of the cards. Still, the mind keeps driving the gambler onward with false hope, and the mind attempts to do the same on a Mission.

There is no break in a Mission for debriefing, and there is no restructuring of the Mission Plan once it is executed, so *we take no chances and play no odds*. In fact, we do the reverse, by working a margin of safety into every move of the Mission. This creates space to compensate for misjudgment and the unexpected.

2. Resistance to Change

On a Mission, errors in judgment occur when we no longer continually adapt to the current situation. I say *continually* because conditions are ever-changing, which demands constant adjustment on our part. This reflects our training motto: *The only constant is change*.

Some people don't believe that conditions are ever-changing. They say that when a Mission goes according to plan, there is no need to adapt, because there is no change. This is erroneous thinking. When I perceive a situation as staying the same, it may seem that way from my perspective because it meets my expectations for how I think it should be. From the greater perspective, nothing is static—everything is always moving and continually adjusting to its ever-changing surroundings. In order to stay attuned to the Mission, we need to do the same.

As soon as we perceive things to be unfolding as expected, we tend to let ourselves relax a bit. When we do, we are no longer fully present and alert. On the other hand, when we function from the awareness that *the only constant is change*, we remain vigilant, with our senses sharp.

It bears repeating: **The only constant is change**.

3. Personal Consciousness

Mission Consciousness is not—and cannot be—*personal consciousness*. The rational mind wants us to think during a Mission: to run scenarios through our expectation, belief, bias, and prior experience mental filters. In addition, our sense organs are preconditioned to create something tangible out of what they perceive. It is these elements that create personal consciousness.

However, none of that has anything to do with the Mission, which is a world of its own. When we rely at all on our personal consciousness in a Mission, we compromise the Mission.

We must maintain Mission Consciousness and use our senses only to serve the Mission. Any organ that thinks or makes decisions autonomously puts the organism at risk because that organ has detached itself. In effect, it has become its own organism.

When this happens, the Mission needs to be aborted and the remaining organs need to realign themselves, so they can again comprise a fully functioning organism. Once that process is achieved, the Mission can continue.

When that is not possible, the pack member or members whose personal perceptions supersede those of the Mission are dropped from the Mission.

4. The Enemy Concept

There is another saying: *Know your enemy.* The beauty of those words lies in the fact that once we know our enemy, he is no longer an adversary. He has become us because we have become him. We know what he thinks and feels; we know what he does and why he does it.

We learn to dwell in his shadow. In doing so, we become invisible to him. We then become capable of neutralizing whatever potential harm he might render. Being unencumbered by conflict and the enemy label, we may even be able to help him recognize that he is us as well.

Once we reach this level of awareness, *know your enemy* becomes *know yourself.* The Awakened Guardian comes to realize that the only real enemy she needs to know is herself.

When we are in limbic resonance—what we call Mission Consciousness—there is no "Hey, this is going well!" or "Uh-oh, I'm screwing up." Our full attention is devoted to the ever-changing now, and our only concern is for the smooth, flawless functioning of the organism: our pack.

The bliss of the Guardian Way comes from immersion in the moment, where we are consumed with a sense of *serving* rather than *achieving.* It gives us a sense of intimate relationship with our pack members and deep rapport with our people.

Chapter 20 Citations

1   "The History of Jigsaw Puzzles" http://www.jigsaw-puzzle-club.co.uk/the%20history%20of%20jigsaw%20puzzles.asp (accessed June 20, 2020)

SETTING UP SHADOW AND STEALTH CAMPS

One of the main occupations of the Guardian is to operate without being seen. This doesn't mean he hides or camouflages himself, but rather he appears without being recognized. For double protection, he emerges where it is least expected. By "he," I am not only referring to the person of the Guardian, but to his associations as well. One of those primary associations is the Guardian Camp.

When we Guardians operate in a remote location, our first priority is to remain mobile. We carry everything we need with us, including gear for cooking and shelter. We then have no attachment to where we have been and no reason to go back. This allows us to remain completely in the now and flexible in terms of where we go next in order to accomplish our Mission.

This focus on mobility contributes significantly to our ability to remain invisible. Without an established rendezvous site or camp, it becomes virtually impossible for anyone in the area to predict where to intercept the pack.

The Shadow Camp

Yet there are times when a semi-permanent camp is necessary, such as when there is only one safe resting site, or when several phases of a Mission are occurring simultaneously and everyone must keep in touch on a regular basis. In such cases, we first set up a *Shadow Camp*, which has all the appearances of a lived-in camp, yet it is only a ruse.

To someone who accidentally stumbles into a Shadow Camp, they will believe it to be our actual camp. The same is true for those with ill intent who are determined to discover us. They will persist until they find something; and when they come across a hearth that looks well used, with a stack of prepared firewood and abundant evidence of foot traffic around the camp, they will quit looking because they will be convinced that they have found us.

Trails lead into the Shadow Camp, ostensibly for the purpose of bringing in firewood, water, and other supplies, and for travel to and from camp. However, we deliberately lay out the trails to intercept anyone in the vicinity and lead them into the Shadow Camp.

The premise we are working with is that when we attract someone *toward* something, we draw him *away* from something else. What he is inadvertently drawn away from in this case is our actual camp: the Stealth Camp.

A Secure Meeting Place

The Shadow Camp is designed to attract people who we expect to show up. Remember that we take no unnecessary risks—not even with our fellow Guardians from other packs. We only share necessary information with them. This is not a matter of trust, but of practicality. Information vital to the Mission must be conveyed clearly and briefly, so that it can be easily remembered and not confused with anything else later. Clarity and succinctness also protect against the information accidentally falling into the wrong hands.

Imagine a Guardian who stays behind in a Mission and is entrusted to give directions to the camp to a second Guardian. If she were given directions to the actual camp and she was intercepted on the way to the camp by someone else, either her direction of travel could give the camp away, or she could be forced to divulge the camp's location.

Instead, the first Guardian is given the site of the Shadow Camp. This way she can neither confuse the two camps, nor will anyone have to worry about her being forced to reveal details about the actual camp. Everyone can rest easier knowing that the only people aware of the Stealth Camp's location are the people actually using it.

When we rendezvous with someone, we meet him at the Shadow Camp, and from there guide him to the Stealth Camp. If it is only a one-time visit, the person will be blindfolded—even if he is a fellow Guardian—so that neither he nor us need to worry about the Stealth Camp being found.

The Stealth Camp

A disguised trail leads from the Shadow Camp to the Stealth Camp, and this is the *only* trail into the Stealth Camp. By calling

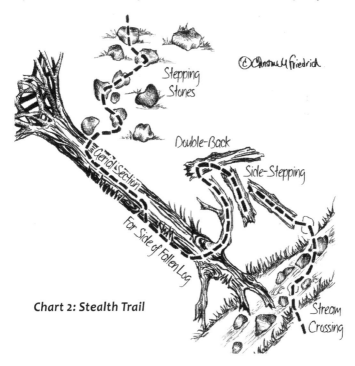

Chart 2: Stealth Trail

it a *trail*, I am using the term loosely, as only the most highly trained Guardians would be able to detect it.

Using stepping stones, double-backs, sections of trail on the far side of fallen logs, sidestepping, aerial sections, and waterways, we construct a "trail" that even we have to use several times in order to fully familiarize ourselves with it. In addition, we choose an unlikely site for a camp, so that outsiders cannot deduce its location.

An everyday camp typically consists of a hearth at the center with firewood stacked conveniently nearby, cooking utensils within easy reach, and a sleeping area and latrine area a skip and a hop away. Just about anyone walking into a typical camp is able to determine pretty quickly that it is a camp, along with ascertaining how well-used it is, how recently it was occupied, and roughly how many people are using it.

Like the stealth trail, the Stealth Camp is only a camp in name. The average person stumbling into it would have no idea it was a camp, so she would walk on, convinced that she came across an isolated hearth, maybe used by some hunters or backpackers passing through; or a stack of firewood, perhaps gathered up and forgotten by someone. Or she may run into a set-up tarp and sleeping bag and see no others in the vicinity, so she will assume that only one person is camping there.

The Stealth Camp, then, has all the components of a typical camp; however, they are dispersed in such a way that each component could pass as a stand-alone feature. In this way, the discovery of one component is unlikely to lead to the discovery of the entire camp.

Another commonly used approach is to hide components of the Stealth Camp from normal view. Firewood could be stacked behind a boulder, and individual sleeping areas might be tucked behind fallen trees or in dense brush. A fire pit on exposed rock can be covered by a boulder when not in use.

One more benefit of a dispersed Stealth Camp is that if it is discovered while occupied, such as by surprise late at night,

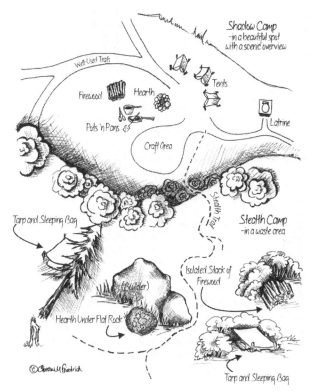

Chart 3: Shadow and Stealth Camps

only one person will be found, and that person will alert the others and set them into action, unbeknownst to the intruders.

As long as the environs of the Stealth Camp show no easily detectible wear, such as trampled trails leading to and fro, there is no reason to move the camp. Scouting for a new location, then camp setup, greatly increase the risk of detection.

Camp Setup Training

In training, both the Shadow Camp and the Stealth Camp are moved regularly so that on a Mission, the Guardians know exactly what to do if the camp must be relocated. If I walk into a training camp and see signs that could easily be detected by a passerby (such as a trail from the hearth to a latrine area or a firewood preparation site within sight of the hearth), the Trainees must immediately abandon the camp. They also need to restore the area so as to leave no trace, then scout for a new camp.

There are no excuses. Training never ends, and they never know when an exercise will morph into an actual Mission—or even if they are already on a Mission. Trainees, as well as established Guardians, must always be prepared and never give in to a false sense of security that could compromise a Mission or the safety of the pack.

I remember walking unannounced into the Stealth Camp of one of my Trainee groups one sunny midsummer afternoon. Along with the wisps of smoke rising from their "smokeless" fire and a shirt hanging up in clear sight from any direction, the stealth trail into the camp became visible because someone had trampled the grass by walking between its steppingstones.

I found the pack members sitting around the fire, eating cantaloupe while cooking their evening meal. They didn't expect me to say anything when I appeared in the clearing, as in the Guardian Way there are no hellos or goodbyes. If there were, someone eavesdropping could easily ascertain the strength of the camp and which pack members were coming or going.

And they didn't expect what I did calmly say, which was "Abort camp."

They knew what to do. Without question, they flew into action. As quickly and discreetly as possible, they had to restore the area of both the Shadow and Stealth Camps to their pristine state. Then they had to scout out the locations for new Shadow and Stealth Camps—and have them set up before dark.

They went to sleep hungry that night. Yet what they did retire with was far more satisfying than a full belly. The next day they shared with each other the deep satisfaction of having the opportunity to show what they were made of—and to come ever closer to being a Guardian worth trusting.

CHAPTER 22

MISSION PLANNING

"**H**ow do I learn the art of planning from the Teachings of Old?" asked a Seeker. "Some say the Ancient Ones know best, as they are to be revered, and I can be inspired by visiting the shrines of their birth and burial. Others say I should avoid their writings and listen instead to the Sages in our midst. I am confused; how should I proceed?"

Her Sage replied, "It is said that Wisdom is timeless, yet many forget that it must also be timely. Much Wisdom stands the test of time, and that is because true Wisdom transcends time. Those who attempt to attach Wisdom to a time, place, or person, are likely confused as to the true nature of Wisdom."

"I am afraid I am one of them," replied the Seeker. "Will you please clarify for me the nature of Wisdom?"

"Think of it as the Path on which we walk the Journey of Discovery. Without Wisdom, there is no Path, and therefore no Journey. The Teachings we garner are the stones that pave our Path. When a Sage suggests that we not read a certain book, it is not because the Wisdom is unsound, but because it is a cobble of a size that does not fit with the cobbles already on our Path. It will trip us up rather than smoothing our way. When the Sage encourages us to seek out a Hermit or listen to the Fool by the roadside, it is because she is one of our Path's missing cobbles."

"I recognize that," replied the Seeker. "Then what about the cobbles that lie ahead? Is it not good to put them in place so that my Path will already be laid out before I get there?"

"That would appear to be the thing to do, for we worry about the future and want the comfort and security of having it planned out before us. However, the present is the death of the future."

"How can that be, when all I have for future preparation *is* the present?" asked the Seeker.

"The Wisdom we now hold only relates to the present," her Sage responded. "When we use it to make decisions for laying out our future, it will only amount to a repeat of the present. The future is our Frontier—it is the unknown. To think of it now will bring up only fear. And that is as it should be, for fear is the music that dances us to our edge, then into the unknown. It is only there—and only then—that we have the presence and perspective needed to choose the cobbles to lay immediately before us."

"What you say overwhelms me," said the Seeker. "I am only barely able to grasp what you describe."

"Think of it as choosing clothes when you were growing up. At age ten, would you have been able to pick out a shirt that would fit when you turned fourteen?"

"Of course not! I now understand: My Path becomes visible only as it unfolds for my next step."[1]

This Zen story has been used since ancient times to teach Mission planning. The Zen approach is to get down to the essence of things. The examples and metaphors in this story give all the vital factors we need to consider. Our remaining task is to flesh out the framework with the details that apply to our particular Mission.

First, the Need for Perspective

In many strategic operations, such as those conducted by the military and other governmental and industrial organizations, the policy is for only the upper echelon of management to have full knowledge of the operation. The reasons are many, but the outcome is the same. The individuals in the lower ranks perform their tasks more successfully without the burden of considering the whole operation. However, this also means that they are ill-equipped to step into another role if it becomes necessary.

This upper/lower echelon system is an ineffective and potentially dangerous management strategy to apply to Guardian Missions. On Missions, each pack member must maintain overall Mission perspective.

Missions are often dangerous and any lack of perspective could mean an injury for a pack member. Contingency plans always take into consideration the possibility that the pack member could be rendered ineffective.

With a well-planned Mission, this does not necessarily mean that the Mission is imperiled or that it has to be aborted. A strong hand can function quite as well with four fingers as five, and the same is true of a well-trained and briefed pack.

No matter how serious the Mission or the degree of risk, it is good practice to fully inform the entire pack of every aspect of the Mission, so that:

- All pack members have the necessary information to adjust to the unexpected.

- Other pack members can fill in for any member taken out of commission.

- Aborted Missions can be quickly reinstated without need for re-briefing.

- Any pack member knows how to set up a diversion or conduct a rescue operation if the situation calls for it.

One exception to the practice of informing the entire pack of all Mission details is the situation discussed in the previous chapter, where there is the risk of a pack member being bugged, tricked, or coerced into divulging sensitive information. Another exception is an otherwise exemplary pack member who is not adept at the art of subterfuge.

Equipping for a Mission

The items a Guardian wears and carries with her on a Mission are just as important as the skills she possesses. A missing tool or interfering item could mean the difference between a successful Mission and putting the pack in danger. Here are the physical basics for every Mission:

- Keep ears uncovered.
- Make sure no visors or ear flaps interfere with peripheral vision.
- Wear quiet clothing appropriate to the Mission.
- Wear quiet, form-fitting footwear.
- Take an extra pair of glasses (for those who wear them).
- Have a piece of all-purpose cordage four body-lengths long.
- Keep a small, all-purpose knife.
- Relieve yourself, whether needing to or not, immediately prior to entering the Mission Site.

Mental and Emotional Preparation

Just as important as physical preparation is the preparation of the self. With the attention to detail that often consumes the pack prior to setting out on a Mission, the most important components of the Mission—you and me—sometimes get overlooked. Here is a personal preparation checklist:

- Be well rested.
- Be completely relaxed and alert.
- Do not carry emotional baggage.
- Always remember that the Mission is life—nothing else exists, nothing else matters.
- Listen, listen, listen.

The Assumptions Trap

One of the most crippling mistakes I see new Trainees make when planning a Mission is making assumptions. Whether right or wrong, an assumption becomes reality as soon as we make it, and then our thoughts and actions become based on that ungrounded reality. I've watched many a Mission fail simply because someone made a foolish assumption. I use the term *foolish* not because it is needed, as all assumptions are foolish, but rather to emphasize the foolish nature of assumptions in general.

Assumptions are answers assumed without first asking the question. To make an assumption directly contradicts a foundational Guardian precept: *Be as a question.*

Recently I went along to drop off our wild rice harvest with the two Ojibwe women who process it for us. Before parching it, they spread it out on tarps in the sun to dry.

"This attracts bears," they said.

"How do you chase them away?" asked someone from our party. "Do you have a dog, or do you use fireworks or something?"

The women smiled, then explained that the bears don't come for the rice, but for the rice worms, who are driven to the edge of the tarp by the hot sun.

"The bears lick up the worms," said one woman, "so they're actually doing us a favor."

Here, as is often the case, the assumption was the direct opposite of reality. The person in our group assumed that the bears were unwanted and would need to be driven away. However, the women wouldn't think of shooing away the helpers who came to do the work that would otherwise fall on them.

Even if avoiding an assumption does not appear to be immediately helpful, it lays the groundwork for actions that could be helpful in the future.

From Assumption to Likelihood

After we stop making assumptions and start questioning everything we approach, there are still no answers, only likelihoods. Where an assumption closes the door to other possibilities, a likelihood leaves the doorway open, which automatically keeps us sharp and discerning.

The next task in our Training, then, is to learn how to establish likelihoods. On a Mission, we need to meet two criteria: speed and reliability. We often have to make split-second decisions, and they have to be solid. We must approach *every* decision, and *every* movement, as though it is critical. This is ultimately because we never know in advance which action is going to be a game-maker or a game-breaker.

Because we are creatures of habit and pattern, the more we get into the groove of likelihoods rather than assumptions, the more natural it is for us to automatically lean toward likelihoods when the pressure is on.

Identifying Likelihoods

We have a method for identifying likelihoods that can be applied to a broad range of situations and decision-making processes, from options under consideration and the directions to take, to relationship issues. The method is based on the following process, and it is called:

The Rule of Three

1. **Choose** a solid observation or idea.
2. **Corroborate** by finding three reliable and unrelated pieces of evidence.
3. **Envision** by running your idea through a scenario to see how it might play out.

We now have a way of identifying something worth pursuing. Remember: Identifying a likelihood by the Rule of Three gives no guarantee of success; it only tips the scale in that direction. You still need to proceed with a *Be as a question* attitude.

Be careful *with the Rule of Three, as we could be tempted to use it to justify a bias or preconceived notion. The Rule works reliably only when we are centered and start with a reasonable option from the perspective of Guardian Consciousness. The same is true with corroborating, as our clever minds could–and would–find a way to corroborate just about anything we want them to corroborate.*

The Last Planning Steps

We've gained perspective from the wisdom tradition of the Guardian Way, we've equipped ourselves and prepared mentally and emotionally, and we've abandoned assumptions for likelihoods. Now we are ready to pull it all together and set out on the Mission that lies before us. Here is how to transition planning to execution.

1. **Assess** the overall situation to reestablish perspective.
2. **Evaluate** all variables to make sure they are accounted for.
3. **Line up** all needed supplies and logistics so that they are immediately accessible.
4. **Come together** in a ritual of unity.
5. **Move out** silently and meditatively.

Make sure each step is complete, flawlessly executed, and done in sequence. If not, go back and perfect the previous step before proceeding to the next one.

In my Trainings and Missions, the Coming Together Ritual is a pack howl. When invisibility is required, our howl is silent. Then we all rub up against each other in an active group hug. It's the same ritual the Wolves and I enacted years ago, just before setting off on a hunt or run.

The ritual triggered something inside each of us that made us feel good about each other and organically connected. Whether we were Wolf or Human didn't matter. We shared the bond of the pack and the lust for the hunt. Those deep and intrinsic characteristics of the Guardian Way ran much deeper than surface identity.

The same is true today in the Coming Together Rituals of my Guardian pack and Trainee packs. There is some magic in the ritual that makes differences between us melt away and the planning process fade into distant memory. All that is left is an all-embracing sense of kinship and an all-consuming dedication to the Mission.

Chapter 22 Citations

1   Tamarack Song, *Zen Rising: 366 Sage Stories to Enkindle Your Days* (Wisconsin: Snow Wolf Publishing, 2017), 86-7.

CHAPTER 23

MISSION EXECUTION

Our pack has trained extensively, and planning is completed. Together we've been careful not to be overconfident because we know it breeds complacency. Yet, a feeling creeps up inside: You start doubting your ability to perform. You feel agitated and a little queasy. It causes you to keep going over the plan to make sure nothing was missed.

Some people call it *the butterflies,* or *stage fright.* The generic term for it is *performance anxiety.* Whatever you call it, the result is the same: crippling. It has to be taken care of *before* moving out on the Mission.

Addressing Performance Anxiety

What triggers performance anxiety is future projecting. It creates a mountain out of a molehill. No longer is executing the Mission a coordinated step-by-step process, but rather everything comes to the forefront at once, and it is overwhelming.

Usually performance anxiety dissipates as soon as we become engaged in the Mission and our instincts take over. However, that can't be trusted, as some people have it so bad that it frays their nerves before the Mission, and during the Mission they end up stuttering and stumbling.

I have found three effective techniques for getting around performance anxiety:

- **Forget about the Mission**. Do something else to take your mind off it. The activity needs to be intellectually engaging: Talk with somebody, read a book, work on a puzzle, play a challenging game. Then when it comes time for the Mission, you'll likely fall right into it since you've been trained to respond instinctively the instant a Mission is called.

- **Deconstruct the Mission**. Every large task is nothing more than a combination of smaller tasks. I can't lift a ton of bricks—or more correctly, *I can't do it if I say I can't*. However, if I take only an armload at a time, I'll have that ton of bricks lifted in short order. All we need to do before and during a Mission is concentrate on what is before us; that's all there is anyway. The Mission is just a mental construct; and if we deconstruct it, we return to the reality of the now.

- **Move like a Bear.** We have a guideline: *In Training, move like a Cat; on a Mission, move like a Bear.* Cats are agile— they jump over and walk atop things instead of on the ground beside them, as Bears do. Being catlike in training develops our capabilities to the maximum. On a Mission however, it can expose us to injury and detection. Instead, we move as a Bear: slowly and deliberately, one step at a time, keeping our feet firmly planted. It may not be very sexy, but it reduces performance anxiety and increases the chances of success by keeping us grounded in the now.

To Aspire Is Dire

When a Mission is going well, there is the temptation to go beyond what is specified in the Mission plan. We start thinking that maybe we can execute it faster, or we can take a shortcut, or we can make off with more than we planned. This desire to aspire is the second most common Mission derailer, right behind performance anxiety.

"In the long run," said Henry David Thoreau, "you hit only what you aim at." On a Mission, this is what we want—the only thing we want—to focus on the task at hand and nothing additional.

The reason is that in the heat of a successful moment, it's highly unlikely that we will consider all of the variables that were previously accounted for in a well thought-out Mission plan. Besides the possibility of not being able to accomplish the additional feat, it is possible that we could jeopardize the entire Mission. When the right hand doesn't know what the left hand is doing, or when the right and left hands are out of sync, anything can happen.

Three More Common Snags

There are a few other lures that inadequately trained Guardians are prone to getting sucked into when executing Missions: luck, gadgets, and improvisation. Here are some strategies for avoiding them:

1. **Don't rely on luck.** On a Mission, all luck is dumb luck. Be conservative. We need to be predictable, reliable, and consistent. *Success comes only from thorough planning and impeccable execution.*

2. **Keep gear minimal.** Plan to execute the Mission with the least amount of equipment possible. *The more gear, the higher the chance of Mission failure.* Use items that can serve multiple purposes. Eliminate duplicity. Utilize your built-in tools—fingers, feet, or teeth—whenever possible before resorting to a packed-in tool.

3. **Utilize what is in-hand or immediately available**. Don't try to fabricate something or break rank to go and get something. Using what is already there saves time and energy and leaves the smallest footprint.

Remember that *any extra motion compromises the stealth aspect of the Mission*. A Mission is a shadow operation, so *we must maintain invisibility at all cost*. That means following all of the guidelines at all times in order to:

- **Assure** the integrity of the Mission.
- **Maintain** reserves of time, energy, and presence for unplanned eventualities.
- **Minimize** detection during and after the Mission.

Buffer Zones for Safety

The reason for calling a Mission, rather than merely conducting a transfer, pickup, or heist, is because of high stakes. A Mission is undertaken with the belief that we have only one opportunity to accomplish it. No margin of safety can be assumed at a Mission Site. Everything has to be executed perfectly, from scouting and signaling to transfer and exit. It is foolish—and sometimes suicidal—to assume that we will be given a second chance if something goes awry.

I have watched some of the most brilliantly planned Missions fail because the pack did not strictly abide by this precept. No matter how stealthy we might think we are, we are still a presence and potentially detectable, so we need to incorporate a margin of safety at every stage of a Mission. When we fail to do this, not only is all the work put into the Mission in vain, but the potential good the Mission could have achieved is lost.

In order to carry out a no-blunder Mission, every movement, line of sight, signal, and point of contact has to have a *Buffer Zone*. Think of a Buffer Zone as the margin of safety needed to accommodate the unexpected and to allow for a margin of error.

Here is a simple example to illustrate the necessity of the Buffer Zone: I knock off my hat when ducking under a branch. Normally I would stop and pick it up; however, I am moving quickly through sensitive territory with my pack and I cannot break formation. The weather is cold, so I run the risk of frostbite *and* I have left behind a sign of our presence. I have compromised the Mission, all because I did not create a Buffer Zone by giving an extra margin of safety when I ducked under the branch.

At the Mission Site there is no room for error. I have to create personal room to assure that my fumbles or adjustments do not have a ripple effect on the Mission. Think of the Buffer Zone as a personal operating space, distinct from the Mission's operating space.

Successful execution of a Mission means more than just pulling it off by the skin of our teeth. In every phase of a Mission, there must be the built-in time and space to accommodate the unexpected. However, this extra space cannot be relied upon on a Mission level. What can be counted on are personal Buffer Zones, which need to be an integral part of Mission planning.

The Importance of Timing

There is a saying that what is important is not *what* we do, but *how* we do it. For the Guardian, there is another consideration: *when* we do it. Timing is easy to overlook, yet it is a vital aspect of stealth and invisibility. I can do everything right. I can move as a shadow and be perfectly coordinated with my packmates, with a foolproof contingency plan set up if things go awry. However, if I make a conspicuous move right when somebody is coming, everything is lost.

In the Guardian Way, only actions speak. Even if I've planned to execute a Mission perfectly by the clock, something will probably disrupt my plan. It doesn't matter if something worked ten times in the past. Worst-case scenarios are always real, and *every* Mission needs to be planned with that contingency in mind. Fortunately, the more we have the timing down, the less chance there is for worst-case scenarios to occur.

For popular culture examples of dispassionate Guardian Consciousness rooted in timing and action, read some Sherlock Holmes or recall the guidance of Star Wars' Yoda. Think of how essential timing is to the hunt, for every Mission is essentially a hunt. It makes no difference whether we are a pack of Wolves after a Deer or a pack of Humans decommissioning a river dam.

Here, our mantra *Only actions speak* comes to the forefront. It is only through active training with real consequences that we can evolve a functional sense of timing.

The Mission in Time

For Guardians on a Mission, engagement is the only thing that exists. Each person's sense of time must momentarily disappear, lest it become distracting. When we practice full engagement in the now, we place ourselves in position for both peak performance and best service to our people.

When something goes wrong, each of us must immediately wipe the slate clean. There is no time to overcompensate for the error or harbor feelings of guilt or regret. Instead, we must immediately adapt to the new scenario and adjust our plan in order to continue with the Mission as seamlessly as possible.

When we don't carry forward this way, we lock ourselves in the past, which creates a time dimension where there previously was none. We then become concerned with how the botched past will affect the future. This is a grave mistake; we become focused on something other than the Mission as it unfolds in the here-and-now. When we are distracted, we lose our sense of presence and awareness—our sharp edge that helps us succeed in a Mission.

Think of a Mission as a fast-paced team game. When a mistake is made, there is no time to reflect and do it over. The mistake needs to be forgotten as soon as it occurs, and an adjustment must be made on the spot. This process occurs seamlessly. When it is done well, all the observer sees is the synchronous flow of the players functioning together in the now, while at the same time methodically advancing toward the shared goal.

In debriefings, only give information relevant to the topic. Time is of the essence—extraneous information distracts and reduces efficiency.

Confidence Kills

"I was so confident this time that I thought for sure I could make a fire," commented a Trainee who was learning to make fire by friction, "but it just didn't work."

Confidence is a killer. If there were guarantees and predictions were infallible, confidence might make sense. But since that's not the case, it's best to just throw confidence out the window. As we discussed, make no assumptions and take nothing for granted. There are always variables we cannot foresee. Being unbridled by assumptions is a core awareness in the Training because it allows us the freedom to envision success and perform beyond our known limitations.

When we lack clear communication, we can fall into the trap of misplaced confidence. Many of us tend to turn to those who we think have the information we need and place our confidence in them. Here, our confidence is in essence a leap of faith. It's like questioning the reliability of someone's car, and she replies, "You can trust it—it's a Ford."

Instead, we need concise, straightforward, and verifiable information. Without it, we must desist until we get it. Being well-versed is the only way we can be fully present and functional pack members. For effective communication training, I recommend my book *Truthspeaking* as an adjunct to this manual. Following are a couple of pointers to get you started.

To answer a question quickly and effectively:

1. Give a clear, succinct reply.
2. Flesh out your answer only if asked or you deem it necessary.

To describe something, present an idea, or give directions:

1. Give a brief, yet thorough explanation.
2. Give two verifiable points of reference.

Think of executing a Mission the way a magician would: making for our audience something visible that already exists.

Our audience is our people, and our goal is to have appear before them what they need. As with the magician's white Dove, what our people need also already exists. All we are doing is helping them see through the imaginary space between them and it. It's the simple secret behind every magician's trick, and it's the simple secret to the success of every Mission. This chapter is essential magician training as well as essential Guardian Training. All we are doing—the magic—is putting the focus on ourselves as the distance between the visible and invisible; then we disappear, and there is no more distance.

KEEPING SILENT AND INVISIBLE

Covertness is one of the defining characteristics of a Mission. It is so important that I would call it the primary pillar upon which a Mission is built. Without covertness, major risks are incurred. Because they take concerted practice to fully develop, covertness skills are well-covered in Guardian Training.

To begin with, let's look at the three levels of Mission execution where failure typically occurs:

1. **Waste of effort.** Any movement that does not contribute directly to the fulfillment of the Mission drains needed focus and energy from the Mission, increasing the chance of detection.

2. **Poor Planning.** The better planned the Mission, the more invisible it becomes. Poor planning is the primary reason for poor execution, which is why no Mission should be undertaken that is not impeccably designed.

3. **Compromised Guardians.** A Mission is just a pipe dream without Guardians. They are the Mission's body and soul. As such they must be capable of functioning beyond the capacity needed for the Mission or they risk being beacons for detection.

Training to Move Like a Shadow

You may be familiar with the Robert Frost poem *The Road Not Taken,* which concludes with these lines:

Two roads diverged in a wood, and I—
I took the one less traveled by,
And that has made all the difference.[1]

In general, it could be argued that Mr. Frost has given good advice. Yet in training, we want to go a step beyond that and not take anything defined at all. In my Guardian Intensive Trainings, we go by this precept: *Stay off all roads and trails, without exception, for the duration of the Training.* Here are the reasons:

1. **Accelerated Training.** I know of no better way to learn how to move swiftly and efficiently than to be forced to find your way through a tangled woods and cross streams on fallen logs.

2. **Personalized Training.** This approach is self-guided, geared to individual need, and accommodates all levels of ability.

3. **Conscious Movement.** When we are forging our own Path, we are knowingly engaged in every step, which is the basis of consistent and accident-free movement.

4. **Thorough Exercise.** All muscle groups are engaged. No two steps are alike, and constant motor adjustments need to be made.

5. **The Unexpected.** Varied and unpredictable terrain forces us to keep our senses sharp and attuned to our surroundings.

6. **Stealth.** Much more so than movement on prepared surfaces, every step carries risk of exposure. Not only foot placement, but what the hands and torso touch, become integral factors in shadow movement.

The same approach can be taken with cross-country skiing or snowshoeing. I particularly like traveling on the edge of a melting snow field; that transitional strip between open ground and snow is typically rugged and unstable.

Even a stroll in the park becomes an exercise when we step off of the walkways. There is doggie-doo to avoid, along with litter, dandelions, and whatever else we want to throw into the mix to challenge us. I find ways to do the same when crossing something as seemingly homogeneous as a paved parking lot. There are oil spots, cracks, painted lines, skid marks, debris, loose gravel, and more to negotiate.

When we are in Guardian Training Consciousness, life is training and training is life. We are then always off-trail, even when we are temporarily on one.

A popular quote often attributed to Ralph Waldo Emerson says, "Do not go where the path may lead. Go instead where there is no path, and leave a trail." The Guardian takes this one step further and leaves no trail.

Invisibility by Decoy

The Least Chipmunk, the smallest of the chipmunk family, is native to the coniferous forests of the Lake Superior bioregion where I live. She ranges west from here, all the way out to British Columbia and California, and down to New Mexico. One unique behavior of hers is to become invisible by sitting perfectly still on her haunches, then flicking her tail and chirping. That sounds about as silly as one of us expecting not to be seen while waving a flag and singing Yankee Doodle, right?

Remember that in the Guardian Way, anything is game—our only criteria are what works. There's another Guardian precept: *It's not what you do, but how you do it, that makes all the difference.* The Least Chipmunk's chirping sounds like a Birdcall, so someone who hears it is going to be looking for a Bird rather than a mammal. In addition, the little Squirrel is a ventriloquist, so where your ears tell you to look is not her location, but the place where she threw her voice.

That's easy enough to understand, but what about that tail flicking? Won't that give her whereabouts away? Yes and no.

If the Bird impersonation and the voice throwing don't work, she needs a backup plan. She knows that many predators are attracted more to movement than to form, so she flicks her tail to attract a predator to it, rather than to her body. Where her tail is hard to grasp and expendable, her body is not.

By using these invisibility tactics, the Least Chipmunk masks her presence and protects herself against predators. Similar tactics can be employed by us to protect both ourselves and the Mission when it is not possible to function completely as a shadow.

Beware of a False Sense of Invisibility

Most of us assume that if we can't see anyone, no one can see us. This gives us a sense of security, because we think we are operating under cover. We then take risks that we would not normally take, assuming our movements will not expose us.

On a Mission, comfort comes only through discomfort. *The more comfortable we feel, the higher our degree of vulnerability.*

If this sounds counterintuitive to you, it is probably your ego talking. The problem is that when we function from our egos, we are centered in our rational minds and guided by our feelings. However, our rational minds are limited by what we know, and our feelings lie to us about the true state of things. This is why we can *think* and *feel* that we are safe when in actuality, we are vulnerable.

Thinking and feeling have no place in a Mission, because a Mission is not about you or me. As soon as we realize that we have involved our egos, we must do one of two things:

- Immediately center ourselves back into Mission Consciousness.
- Bow out of the Mission.

If we don't choose one of those options, we imperil both ourselves and our pack members. And we compromise the Mission, which reduces its chance of success.

When we enter Guardian Consciousness, our egos—along with their controlling thoughts and feelings—take a back seat for two important reasons. First, this is the only way we can remain *Selfless, Alert, and Safe* (SAS)—the three states of being each pack member *must* achieve in order to participate in a Mission. Second, ego-less being is the only way we can remain uncomfortable enough to make sure we are truly invisible. Otherwise, we are constantly fighting our egos, whose main goal is to seek comfort for us.

Our egos cannot be trusted to set aside their own desires. They will lie and cheat to achieve their ends, because for them, there is nothing dishonest about it. They are designed to function above and aside from all ethics and consideration for others. Don't get me wrong, this is a natural and important process—but only in its place, which is *not* on a Mission.

When Stealth Is Harmful

Many Trainees hold stealth as the pinnacle of Guardian action. Above all else, they strive to be surreptitious, and they want to maintain covertness on a Mission. They think stealth, they train for stealth, and they incorporate stealthy maneuvers into their Mission planning.

However, there are times when stealth is not only unnecessary, but detrimental. The rule of thumb is, **When there is no reason for stealth or when you are not confident that you can maintain stealth, be blatant**. Some of the reasons for blatancy include:

1. It doesn't raise suspicion.
2. It offers the cloak of legitimacy.
3. We can convincingly plead ignorance if we are accused.
4. It provides cover when needed.

We are fooled by blatancy all the time; we just don't recognize it. We don't notice a thief taking something right before our eyes because we can't imagine anyone having the gumption to do so. We automatically suspect someone who runs from the scene of a crime, but we hardly ever suspect the person who reports the crime. Conducting a successful Mission requires a Guardian to know the time and place for both stealth and blatancy.

Mission Silence

Precision and brevity in communication are essential to the success of a Mission. As previously discussed, when messages are transmitted clearly and quickly, all phases of the Mission go more smoothly. The two arenas of communication are *internal* and *external*.

Internal Communication is information sharing within the pack, and here is how to conduct it successfully.

- Keep details as precise as possible.
- Maintain overall Mission perspective.
- Be sure that each pack member receives all of the information relevant to her particular function.
- Be careful of giving out any unrelated information, which tends to confuse and get in the way of Mission execution.
- Think adaptability, which is best supported—especially in high-stress situations—by a well-informed pack.

The more complex the Mission, the less necessary it is for all pack members to have a full grasp of the Mission. The planners must determine how much each pack member needs to know in order to adapt in worst-case scenarios, but not divulge Mission-compromising information if he is captured.

External Communication is information sharing with anyone potentially exposed to the Mission but not directly related to it. Here are the variables to keep in mind:

- For anyone outside the pack, the official line—for stealth purposes—is that there is no Mission. The only exception is a necessary adjunct, who is given only the information necessary to perform his role.

■ For all others who will potentially be exposed, the best smokescreen is no smokescreen. It keeps the pack sharp and increases the odds of a successful Mission.

■ Every bit of leaked information that is not essential to the execution of the Mission greatly increases the chances of outside interference.

People indirectly involved in the Mission, such as those who might be exposed to some phase of the Mission in operation, and those who are asked to clear out of the Mission zone, need to know enough about the Mission to be able to support it. Any information beyond that greatly increases the risk of exposure. The details that need to be known by as few people as possible are:

■ The full purpose of the Mission

■ Mission organizers

■ Pack members and their identities

■ The time of the Mission

■ The means by which it is to be executed

■ Potential collateral damage

The Folly of Smokescreens

It is commonly believed that a smokescreen should be used to either mask or distract attention from a Mission. I am not an advocate of these tactics. Pulling off an effective smokescreen is a Mission itself. Its failure–or even the glimmer of suspicion that it might raise–indicates that something surreptitious is happening.

How Your Face Speaks Louder Than Words

Nonverbal cues can either negate or reinforce what I communicate verbally. If I am spinning a convincing yarn, yet the interrogator sees tension in my face, there's a good chance she'll see through my story. The best way to not betray my story with my body is to *keep a loose jaw.* Rather than pursed lips, tensed jaw muscles, and puckered cheeks, my face will look relaxed and my story will be more believable.

Our physical state is intrinsically connected to our emotional state. When we are feeling stressed or anxious, our posture rigidifies and our muscles tighten up. The reverse is true as well: When our muscles are tense or strained, we tend to feel on-edge emotionally. We can use this to our advantage in creating a mask. With a loose jaw, we feel and look more relaxed. Here are some tips for keeping a loose jaw:

- Keep some space between your upper and lower teeth at all times. When they are touching, your jaw is not loose.

- Whenever you clench your teeth, rotate your jaw to relax it.

- When anxious or under stress, check to see if your jaw is relaxed. If not, rotate it immediately to loosen it up.

- Before entering a stressful situation, loosen your jaw.

- Loosen your jaw periodically throughout the day, whether or not it is clenched.

After you have practiced this exercise for a period of time, you will notice that your jaw—and face—remain naturally relaxed when tension rises. It is important to reach this point with the exercise since the last thing you want to do in the middle of an interrogation is rotate your jaw to help relax yourself, as it would be a dead giveaway.

A Re-centering Technique

In executing our duties as Guardians, there will inevitably be times when we feel awkward in front of others, or exposed and out of place. Any sign of disjointedness on our part could expose us and our Mission. There is no reason for this if we train to avoid it. Here are three quick steps to maintain your shadow presence:

1. **Don't react.**
2. **Center yourself.**
3. **Align your energy** *with the one who is making you feel uncomfortable.*

Now we are ready for the next level of training, which is mixing blatancy with stealth. Blatancy creates a focal point for the unsuspecting, to keep them unsuspecting. At the same time, it provides an extra veil of safety for those who need to stay covert during the Mission.

However, blatancy and stealth are diametrically opposed tactics; each takes a separate skill set and frame of mind. I consider only the Guardians who have progressed in training to this point to be capable of learning what is involved to be both blatant and stealthy in the same Mission.

The subject matter of the next chapter is a prime example of the dichotomy. Ostensibly, the chapter is about how to protect both yourself and the Mission if you are discovered. Yet one tactic that creates a delicate Balance between blatancy and stealth is creating a diversion by allowing yourself to be discovered. This instills a false sense of confidence and accomplishment in your captors, which allows you to "break down" and feed them false, diversionary information. At the same time, to distract them from the Mission, you can compromise them by stroking their egos and surreptitiously undermining their belief systems.

I cannot overstress how important the next chapter is to your Training. You are entering a dimension of performance that takes you beyond straightforward stealth and prepares you for what may be the most labyrinthian psychological playing field for a Guardian.

Chapter 24 Citations

1   Robert Frost, *Mountain Interval* (New York: Henry Holt and Co., 1916), 9.

CHAPTER 25

WHEN DISCOVERED ON A MISSION

If a pack member or support person is discovered and questioned, the rule of thumb is to not give out any information. This does *not* mean remaining silent, as doing so immediately confirms that we are involved in something surreptitious. This puts both ourselves and the Mission in jeopardy. Instead, take either of these approaches when confronted:

1. **Relax and talk.** Do it in that order. Nervousness speaks more than what you say. One has to be relaxed in order to talk in a free-flowing manner. The more we talk, the more we are going to divert attention from the fact that we are not saying anything of value. Our goal is exactly that: talk a lot without saying anything. People are used to this because it's what most of us do anyway, so it will not raise suspicion. What typically happens is that we either bore the person or she comes to realize that we really don't have any valuable information for her.

2. **Defer to a greater authority.** This is the fallback option when it is clear that the first approach is not working. Start by playing dumb: You are only doing what you are told. You don't know why you're here, but someone else surely does, and your interrogator would serve herself much better by talking to that other person.

   Here we have three choices:

   a. **Give our inquisitor a fictitious person in authority to contact.** This is the best option when we just need to buy enough time to conclude the Mission. Be careful here because if you are re-questioned later, you want to be able to explain away your fictitious authority figure as a simple—and believable—mistake.

b. **Defer to an authority unaware of the Mission.** If this is executed well, it amounts to a double cover-up, which buys extra time. After finding and consulting the authority, your inquisitor could think the authority (who of course will deny any involvement) is lying to protect himself.

c. **Defer to the authority predetermined to handle a cover-up** by putting up a rehearsed smokescreen. This is the least favorable option because it implicates another person. Nevertheless, it is the best option when either *choice a* or *choice b* are not possible.

Be Careful when Using Fictitious Authorities

When our inquisitor is a law enforcement officer, defer to a fictitious authority only when necessary. The judicial system takes a dim view of any behavior that makes officers' jobs more difficult. In my state (Wisconsin), such an act could be considered Obstructing an Officer, a Class A misdemeanor carrying a fine of up to $10,000 and nine months in jail.

The details of *deferring to a greater authority* need to be discussed in the Mission planning phase. If more than one person is apprehended and they are questioned separately, their stories need to match. In addition, not all people can switch quickly and smoothly from Mission Consciousness to the consciousness of the apprehender. Planning for a stressful situation like this will help ease that transition.

Avoid Cover-up Stories

For the sake of Mission security, throw out the concept of the cover-up story. Even though alibis, excuses, and self-justifications are standard fare in book and movie mysteries—and sometimes in our own lives—they are not effective.

The reason? A cover-up story sounds like, well, a cover-up story. To the astute person, it comes across as phony already with the first few words. The reasons are that we sound rehearsed, we are too earnest, or we project an exaggerated sense of sincerity. If that doesn't do it, we often end up backpedaling to keep our story sounding believable.

The second risk is that our cover-up story can further incriminate us. If we don't get some facts right or our inquisitors know something we don't think they know, we are caught obviously lying. At that point, there is nothing we can do to rescue ourselves, and the Truth will inevitably surface.

So let's keep the suspense—and the risk—that cover-up stories generate for the movies and books. Neither suspense nor added risks have any place in real Missions. Besides, we have safer alternatives.

Context Is Everything

Whenever possible when a Mission is exposed, it is best to explain what is actually going on. Only when there are legal, safety, or strategic issues are cover-ups of any kind recommended. Training Missions, though, are a different story, as we take nearly everything to the extreme for the sake of the Training.

What to Do If You Are Discovered

1. **Act clueless**. You don't know what happened or when it happened. If you saw something or engaged in something, it was just coincidental because you were only passing

through. Besides, you couldn't be at the scene of the incident because you didn't realize there *was* an incident.

2. **Let the inquisitor tell the story.** You're clueless and he wants information, so in order to get it, he's going to have to go fishing. In doing so, he is in essence creating a story, which you can adopt to hide behind.

3. **Don't deny anything**. Denial is as easy to read as guilt. You could very well have seen something, but that doesn't mean you understood what you saw. You could definitely have touched something, and they might have your fingerprints to prove it; however, it may have just been in passing. Your inquisitor won't tell you that other people might have seen or touched the same thing, and his task is to ferret out the person who did it with intent.

4. **Don't sound defensive.** You won't if you adopt the mindset that you did nothing wrong and have nothing to hide or defend.

5. **Be curious.** Show surprise at what they reveal. Ask questions and sound genuinely interested.

6. **Align with the inquisitor.** The reason he's questioning you is that he has a belief system that gives clear parameters as to what is right and wrong. Identify with the belief system and you may touch a resonant chord with him. Yet be careful about aligning with his story, as that may raise contradictions and suspicions. Make your resonance sound genuine by finding something inside yourself that is honestly in alignment with his belief system. He will then feel not only your empathy, but a sense of kinship that goes beyond words and the issue at hand.

If you execute the previous six points satisfactorily, there is a good chance that your inquisitor will let you go. He will either be convinced that you are innocent, or he will still be suspicious but not able to get enough traction to pin anything on you. Either way, you've served both your pack and the Mission by maintaining the Mission's integrity and not incriminating your pack. If you were found to be involved in the incident, it would have meant guilt by association for your entire pack.

When All Else Fails

Let's say that the diversionary tactics we have covered didn't work. We are now down to our last resort—the alibi. We wanted to avoid it at all costs because it carries the most risk. Whenever we have to contribute something to a suspicious inquisitor, everything we say—and how we say it—is going to be scrutinized and possibly held against us later.

The way around this is to tell our story without telling a story. Forget about an introduction, a plot line, and a conclusion. Here's how to do it:

- **Make the story sound spontaneous,** simply by being spontaneous. Make up details as you go. You will then naturally sound unrehearsed, without an agenda or something to prove.

- **Go on tangents.** That is, go on what *sound* like tangents to the interrogator. We naturally do this when we talk, so your inquisitor will expect this over a well-rehearsed story that is straight to the point. Talk about items of interest that you can back up with authentic facts and your own personal history.

- **Weave actual incriminating facts into the story**—but only as sidelines. They need to be incidental to the story, so just mention them matter-of-factly, within the context of your rambling.

No matter the direction that the questioning goes, and no matter the result, our state of mind means everything. If we feel guilty and accused, we're going to look suspicious and act defensively. Instead, we want to be surprised and curious. There's no reason to tighten up and start sweating if we are in the driver's seat. Remember, our inquisitor is just fishing. If he doesn't come up with true evidence or a warrant that means he doesn't have enough information and he is simply trying to dig up more.

Play his game and there's a good chance you will lose because you are playing by his rules. You need to make it *your* game. The trick is to not let him know what game or whose game he is playing. If you can do that by using the guidelines in this chapter, you'll buy time and may even save the Mission.

CHAPTER 26

EFFECTIVE STEALTH SIGNALING

Near the top of the list of essential Mission skills is signaling. Certainly signaling is the backbone of any Mission and the nervous system of the pack; it keeps all of the organs connected and functioning seamlessly. Any breakdown in signaling immediately compromises the Mission.

Signaling is so critical that when I or another staff member detect a blatantly obvious signal during a Mission Training, we abort the Mission. This carries immediate consequences for the Trainees, which sometimes means they go without food for a day or more. The pack receives food every few days at a predetermined location on a forest road near their camp. They conduct their food pickups as stealth Missions by positioning Scouts up and down the road and selecting a food processing site that is invisible from the road (see illustration on the following page).

Only one person in the pack should ever be seen, and that is the one who comes up to the car to remove the food from the trunk. She has an alibi rehearsed in case anyone comes by and asks what's going on, in order to disguise the existence of the pack and its camp.

After she unloads the food, she passes it on to someone hidden behind a boulder or roadside brush, who then passes it on to the next person, and so on, until it reaches the processing site. If we see anybody other than her—and that includes signalers and their signals—during setup or execution of the Mission,

Chart 4: Food Mission

we immediately leave, even if they have not yet unloaded any of the food.

Perfecting Mission Signals

From *stealth perspective*, there is no distinction between signal and signaler. A signal is an extension of the signaler—they are one. Think of the signal as a living appendage, just like an arm or a leg. In this way, the signal is imbued with the spirit and consciousness of the signaler.

When the signaler separates herself from the signal, she loses conscious connection with the Mission. The odds are greatly increased of the signal standing out and becoming detectable, even though the signaler remains camouflaged. If the signal is detected, the person is detected, and the Mission is compromised.

Let's take a look at what it takes to send and receive an operative signal.

The Four Criteria of an Effective Signal:

1. Discreet.

- It fits seamlessly into both the environment and the situation.

- It is detectable only by the signal receiver.

- It is so subdued that the receiver must be acutely attentive to catch it.

2. Precise.

- It is simple.

- It has one clear meaning only.

- It cannot be confused with any other signal.

3. Verified.

- It is not complete until the signaler receives a "message received" signal in return.

- The "message received" signal is just as precise as the signal itself.

- The "message received" signal has to clearly come from the intended receiver.

4. Fast.

- It comes soon after the reason for signaling.

- The "message received" signal follows immediately.

When There Is No "Message Received" Verification:

1. **Assesses** the signal execution.
2. **Resend** the message, making any necessary changes to improve clarity.
3. **Freeze** the Mission until the message is completed.
4. **Abort** the Mission, when:
   - The signal cannot be completed after several attempts
   - The time taken compromises the Mission

The Qualities of a Signal

A stealth signal should be so subtle that even the trained eye has to look twice to detect it. If the Scout's signal is being picked up consistently by other Scouts, the signaler is not in training mode and dancing out on her edge.

A missed signal is the signaler's teacher. She needs to figure out why the signal was missed, while at the same time not making her signal more conspicuous.

From stealth perspective, it doesn't matter whether signals are audible or visual. All that matters are the four criteria for an effective signal. The type of signal is chosen to fit both the Mission and the setting. On a windy day, or when all is quiet, a visual signal might be more appropriate than an audible signal. At night, or when there is no line of sight, an audible signal would be more fitting.

All communication on a Mission is two-way. It has to be for the sake of confirmation, as any missed signal could imperil a Mission. The return signal, which is a confirmation that the signal has been received and registered, needs to be either the same signal (to affirm that the signal was properly read), or a different prearranged signal.

If any signal comes across to the receiver as being too obvious, the receiver immediately sends a "too loud" signal back to the signaler. The reply must be distinctive and immediate:

distinctive so that it does not get confused with any other message, and immediate in order to be effective. The signaler can recognize what went wrong with her signal and correct it.

The Consciousness of the Signaler

It is stealth that makes a Scout a good decision maker. That means the Scout needs to stop thinking and hand over her mind to the Mission. Otherwise the Scout injects her preferences, beliefs, and limitations into the Mission's consciousness, and they become the preferences, beliefs, and limitations of the Mission.

A common error that Trainees make early on is to come from *ego perspective* rather than stealth perspective. That spells danger for the Mission, no matter what role the Trainee is playing. In the Scout role, the ego-centered Trainee can be perfectly camouflaged and may think she is undetectable, and then give an obvious signal—like waving a branch on a perfectly still day. If that Scout were operating in *Stealth Consciousness*, and if she were Mission-centered rather than ego-centered, such an action would be as unthinkable as poking out her head and waving her hand.

When we are in Stealth Consciousness, we automatically consider outside risk factors by looking through the eyes of the potential discoverer. When we are in ego consciousness, we look through our own eyes, and that's where our ego and personal limitations come together to compromise the Mission.

Take the case of a Scout who prefers visual signals because they are clearer and less detectable than audible signals. Yet, if the potential discoverer were a typical adult, 85 percent of his sensory input would be visual, so he would be more likely to pick up a visual rather than an audible cue. At night, the reverse would be true. However, these considerations typically escape the Scout viewing the situation from ego perspective.

A Training Tip

A good ratio of received-to-missed signals for the signaler to strive for is two-to-one. This creates a dynamic tension that keeps both the signaler and the signal receiver on their toes, yet the failure rate is not high enough that it will significantly hinder the Mission. Constant success in signaling is the enemy of a successful Mission. There must be failure in signaling in order to assure both a Mission's overall success and the continued growth and refinement of the Scouts' signaling skills.

Stripping Communication to the Bone

Ideal communication amongst pack members occurs at a glance. The information conveyed needs to be intuitive and instant. This is essential for moving like a shadow and maintaining Mission invisibility.

Communication assessment is a regular part of training and Mission debriefings. We regularly look for ways to reduce our communication imprint by decreasing audible and visual cues, as well as looking at the time taken to send and receive messages.

Here are the four risks of lengthy communication in order of importance. The longer a message takes to be transmitted,

1. The more it disrupts the flow of the pack
2. The higher the possibility of misinterpretation
3. The greater the chance of interception
4. The higher the likelihood of it being interrupted by environmental factors

At one training camp, the pack attempted to address these risks by developing five distinct calls for the different reasons they had to come together:

- Emergency
- Meeting
- Mealtime

* Training run

* Take your time, but let's get together soon.

That sounds pretty evolved, right? But did their signals meet the criteria of being intuitive and instant? In order to find out, I posed some questions to the pack: "If one of you were to put out an emergency call, would you be certain that all of your packmates would respond intuitively and instantly?"

They weren't sure.

My next question: "What if the call went up at night when you were sleeping, or in an extreme condition such as a storm or flood?"

Again, they weren't sure.

The final question: "What if you weren't able to clearly hear the call?"

This time, they were quite sure that their responses would not be intuitive or instant.

The main glitch in their approach was that when a packmate heard a call, he would have to determine which call it was, if he heard it right, and how important it might be. He did so to decide when, if, and how fast he would respond—a process that was anything but intuitive and instant.

The pack concluded that they needed to train for only one call. In this way, they realized, they could best prepare themselves to bolt for the rendezvous point without thinking, no matter what the reason, time, or environmental factors.

At that point, their Training began in earnest.

The Ultimate in Stealth Signaling

Quintessential communication, whether it is in training, on a Mission, or just around camp, is the transfer of information that looks like anything but the transfer of information. If someone notices the signal, the best-case scenario is that it will go undetected by others. The second-best scenario is that it will be interpreted as something other than a signal.

Here are a couple of examples:

1. I'm at the beach, gazing out at the sunset over the water. No one would suspect anything of this perfectly normal and innocent activity. And no one would think twice about whether or not I was barefoot, standing near the water, leaning on a boulder, or sitting down.

2. A stick lies beside the trail. It's in a wooded area with overhanging tree branches, so passersby wouldn't give it any more notice than they would the other dead branches littering the ground.

The first scenario allows for effective stealth signaling for two reasons: The message can be picked up at a glance, and there are four levels of communication occurring simultaneously. They are:

■ The fact that I am there

■ Whether or not I am barefoot

■ My location on the beach

■ My posture

Here is the translation of the previously agreed-to code: My presence indicates that the Mission is on, my barefootedness says that no additional pack members are needed, my position out where the waves lap the beach means that we will use the northernmost prearranged rendezvous site, and the fact that I am sitting on a boulder shows that I will stay behind as a Scout to protect the rendezvous site.

How's that for instant communication? Imagine how many words and how much time it would take to convey all of that verbally. As we discussed in *Stripping Communication to the Bone*, the more time a signal takes, the higher the risk of detection, misinterpretation, and interruption.

Still, there is a glitch: my presence. Any time a pack member is exposed, he and the Mission are vulnerable, for these reasons:

■ His presence and location are known.

- It is far safer and easier to maintain invisibility than to again have to become invisible in order to move as a shadow.

- He could be linked to the Mission if it were discovered.

- He may not be able to create an alibi.

- He could be forced or tricked into exposing the Mission and revealing details.

The second scenario carries all the benefits of the first, with none of the risk. A seemingly random stick lying on the ground bears no relationship to human activity. Yet that stick can be just as expressive as I was in the first example, with just as many levels of communication occurring simultaneously. We can vary the stick's length, the number of side branches, the direction in which it lies, and whether or not it has leaves.

Another important benefit to the second approach is that a pack member who would otherwise be tied up signaling is available to serve in other ways.

The Three Core Concepts for Ultimate Stealth Signaling

1. It in no way resembles signaling.
2. There are no people involved.
3. It is completely disguised as merely one of many similar on-site features.

Throughout the book, you have seen many references to my Teaching Drum Guardian Trainings and to Missions that I have participated in or coordinated. I wrote this book as a training manual for those experiences. At the same time, I structured the book to be a complete at-home training manual. With it, you can progress either alone or with others, and you can conduct your own Missions.

For additional support and inspiration—and further instruction—you can participate in the Trainings I offer and join an online Guardian group.

CHAPTER 27

NEUTRALIZING SOMEONE WHO BRANDISHES A WEAPON

We've all heard sayings like *Violence begets violence* and *Those who live by the sword shall die by the sword*. Recent studies show that these are not just quaint old maxims, but facts of life. The odds of a person being shot are 4.5 times greater if he carries a gun, and his odds of being killed are 4.2 times greater.[1] Even if he doesn't get shot, his chances of coming out on top of the conflict are slim, just because he is *carrying* a gun.

This can be explained in part by the victim's mental attitude. Another study shows that drivers who carry weapons are 44 percent more likely to make obscene gestures at other drivers and 77 percent more likely to aggressively follow another motorist.[2]

I know—choosing to face an armed assailant without a weapon defies logic, contradicts gun lobby propaganda, and runs against much self defense, martial arts, and military training. But the Guardian Way is about results—it's about protecting our people—which is why I teach what works rather than what's popular.

An Assault-Survival Strategy

It is not the Guardian Way to get involved in violent confrontations, whether or not there are weapons involved. Yet it can happen—or we could come upon someone else being assaulted—so in order to protect ourselves and serve our people in such situations, we must train in violent confrontation strategies. Here are the first two steps for not only surviving but transforming such situations:

Step 1 – Don't carry a weapon. It makes us less likely to be aggressive, trigger our assailant's aggression, or get injured or killed. Choosing not to carry a weapon puts us in the best position to use our stealth weapon, which is …

Step No 2 – Use your mind. It is the greatest possible weapon, as it:

- Is more powerful than any person, fighting technique, or weapon
- Gives better odds of prevailing
- Carries less risk
- Is easier to conceal
- Creates less immediate and long-term fallout

The majority of violent acts are not the result of the initial confrontation, but rather of follow-up or revenge attacks. If we win a conflict, that means there's a loser; and if we don't kill him, he could become a sore loser and hurt us in the future. After all, he is an aggressor, and nearly all aggressors function from their egos.

Even if we do kill our adversary, we still have to watch our backs, as he likely had family and friends, and they might try to avenge his death. This is how violence begets violence.

The Power of the Mind

Since ancient times, it has been known that the mind is the ultimate weapon. Take this traditional Zen story:

A man was a fabled wrestler and Guardian of his people, and he had grown old. Yet aspiring young Guardians still came to learn by sparring with him, and he never tired of the game.

One day a young man came who did not have the look of wanting to learn in his eyes. "I will defeat you," he hissed to the Elder Guardian. "No one has been able to best me, and I doubt that a wrinkled old fart like you will be the first."

The Trainees who had gathered round whispered to each other, "That gorilla will kill our venerable Teacher. We must talk him into refusing the challenge."

Even though the Aged One heard their talk, he stepped forward with an air of serenity and said to the visitor, "I consider it an honor to accept your challenge."

First assessing each other, the two grapplers then positioned themselves to take full advantage of the one who made the first move. The young stud growled and spit in the Elder's face. He cursed the Elder's mother and kicked dirt at him, which stuck to the spit. Still, the Elder remained as centered as when he first greeted the challenger.

This went on for half of the morning, until the challenger finally realized he had a formidable opponent. Or more accurately, he had no opponent. Yet as much as the rival needed to win, he would not attack. He knew it would make him vulnerable to even an old man, as all the Elder would have to do is turn the energy of the attack back upon itself.

There was one insult the challenger knew would work. It was now all or nothing; he could not go home and face the jeers that would come after being defeated by an old man. The young buck took off his sash, stood naked in front of the serene Guardian, and peed on the Guardian's feet. Tensed and ready for a lightning response, the young man took a quick step back.

Feeling the heat of combat course through his body, he studied the Elder's form, looking for any sign of tightness or twitching that would indicate a reaction. The Elder's face showed nothing but tranquility.

The pompous one gingerly backed away, and when he felt it was safe to turn around, he turned and ran down the road.

"How could you stomach such abuse for so long?" asked a voice in the crowd.

"Why didn't you teach him a lesson?" asked another, and many similar questions came flying rapidly at the Balanced One.

After everyone relaxed and quieted, he finally spoke: "When someone offers a gift and it is not accepted, whose gift is it?"

In a combat situation, we are psycho-emotionally designed to turn control of our beings over to our egos, whose main jobs are self-protection and self-promotion. We Guardians, on the other hand, train to keep centered in our Heart-of-Hearts, so that we have complete access to all of our capacities and to all options. The story gives us metaphors for both approaches to combat, and now we learn how to effectively use the second one.

The Mental Mastery Method

Let's get right down to how to be the "victor" in confrontation with someone who is wielding a weapon. First, I need to state again that *the way to win is by not winning*—by not creating a loser who will go on being vengeful. The method I outline does not challenge the assailant's ego, nor does it overpower him, which is why both the long-term and short-term risks are greatly reduced. Here is how it is done:

1. **Respect the weapon.** Our assailant will interpret this as having respect for him, as he sees his weapon as an extension of himself.

2. **Determine the real weapon** by searching for why he is actually coming at us. Is it fear? Need? Desperation? Prejudice? Jealousy?

3. **Align with the real weapon**, the one we have just determined.

For #3, let's use the example of an assailant who has a need for money to support his drug habit. You reply, "I feel for you brother, I just got out of treatment last year. I wish I brought some real money with me to help you out. Here, I'll give you what I have on me, then let's go to the ATM up the street so I can get you some *real* money!" Aligning with his energy and the promise of more of what he is after could save your life, and it buys you time to figure out an escape. Even if no escape is possible and the ATM doesn't give you any money, your assailant still has what he was initially after, and you may have created enough empathy for him to just let you go.

The Danger of Bluffing

Bluff only if you can back it up when your bluff is called or if you have a sure escape route. Otherwise, you run a high risk of infuriating your assailant if he calls your bluff, which would put you in a worse predicament than where you started.

Breaking the Ego-Response Pattern

There is no difference between one person fighting another and one army fighting another. If we use violence to settle interpersonal conflicts, we will do the same with group conflicts. We are designed to be creatures of habit.

It takes concerted and consistent effort to abandon old patterns and reawaken our intrinsic conflict resolution skills. The process reveals one of the deeper meanings to our saying that

Life is training and training is life. In fact, the best way to relearn Mental Mastery is to make it your life.

To Live Mental Mastery

1. **Refuse to argue.** It forces you to both listen and express yourself effectively.

2. **Do not acknowledge conflict.** Look instead for the hidden resonance, which is always there.

3. **Live with mentally skilled people.** By associating with them, you automatically absorb the techniques of Mental Mastery.

4. **Offer to mediate others' conflicts.** It's easier to see things in others than in yourself. In addition, the final test of skill mastery is demonstrating and teaching it to others.

When the Mental Mastery Method Fails

Here we get into slippery territory. Whether I personally succeed or fail is not the main concern, but rather the success of the Mission—and even more so, the good and welfare of my people (which is my overall Life Mission that I am participating in with every breath). How I view my own performance is important only to my pesky ego. My "failure" could bring about the Mission's success. Just as well, the failure of the Mission might ultimately be for the good of the people.

Here is a traditional Zen Guardian story that demonstrates the folly of labeling anything a success or failure by its apparent outcome.

A man served his ruler well, so the ruler wanted to reward him with something meaningful. One morning the man, who had to walk wherever he went, woke up to a new carriage outside his door, pulled by a team of perfectly matched Horses.

"What a stroke of fortune!" his neighbors called out when they passed by. "You must feel like the luckiest man on Earth."

"Perhaps," was the man's only reply.

A week or so later while taking his new carriage down a country lane, he met a man in an oxcart coming from the opposite direction. The oxcart swerved and drove the carriage off the road. It flipped and tumbled down the steep embankment. The oxcart driver pulled the man out of the wreckage, laid him in the oxcart, and took him to a nearby inn, where he could stay until his broken bones were mended enough to make the trip home.

The next day when the man's friends heard of the accident, they came to visit him at the inn. "What an unfortunate soul you are," they said to him. "Of all things to befall you—especially after such a stroke of luck with getting the carriage."

Even though he was in extreme pain, the man looked into his friends' eyes, and with a slight smile replied, "Maybe."

A few days later, his friends came by again with news: "There was a heavy rain up on the mountain that triggered a mudslide in the middle of the night. It took your house, which went crashing into the rocks in the valley below. Aren't you lucky that you were here safe in bed?"

Personal responsibility starts long before the actual confrontation. The carriage driver in the story didn't decide to be as a question and remain open to all possibilities at the time of his crisis. Rather, for him it was a way of life, which is why he could remain centered and not only see, but benefit from, all in life that was seemingly beyond his control. It is an approach to life that the indigenous Elders who trained me call the *Beauty Way*.

The reason we do not live and serve in the Beauty Way, as does the carriage driver, is because—again—we are creatures of habit and pattern. Like the carriage driver's friends, how we respond when the pressure is on is how we respond when there is no pressure.

Breaking the pattern that keeps the gate to the Beauty Way locked is the reason to start training *now* and to *always* be in training. It's the one approach that works because every thought and movement is going to either help us progress or cause further regression. There is no in-between. Think of it as *Prevention Training* because we are preventing the usual (like the carriage driver's friends) helplessness-victimization responses to confrontations and crises.

The Four Cornerstones of Prevention Training

Imagine how the carriage driver would handle being confronted by a weapon-wielding person, then imagine how his friends would handle the same situation. What they lack is given in the following Four Cornerstones. Please note: You will make the most progress with the Four Cornerstones if you do them in conjunction with the *To Live Mental Mastery* approach in the previous section.

The Four Cornerstones

1. **Foresight.** If I keep a spare key secured behind the bumper of my car, I won't get caught out in a parking lot in the middle of a rainstorm when I lose my car keys. The Mental Mastery Method covers the majority of confrontational situations, so we may never have to take the spare-key risks of getting physical with someone.

2. **Mind the mind.** If we train primarily to meet aggression physically that is likely what will happen in a confrontation. If we train to align with aggressive energy in order to defuse it, we can expect that to happen during a confrontation. What we feed, grows, so if we start with Mental Mastery Training, it'll save our skin many times more often than physical training ever could.

3. **Learn from Nature.** Watch the animals, who continually work out conflict and align energies with very little

physical contact. They can't afford to risk injury, as they need to maintain prime physical condition in order to survive. I lived with a pack of Wolves and watched them regularly work things out with Mental Mastery. Only once in that time did one injure another, and I was largely to blame.

4. **Train for physical confrontation.** Even with solid Mental Mastery Training, a worst-case scenario might still occur. Flashy fight moves might look impressive in a movie or training set-up, yet in real life they could fall short. Train instead in methods that are:

- **Adaptable.** They are more reliable than those geared toward specific scenarios.

- **Instant.** The longer they take, the greater the risk.

- **Stealthy.** They are inherently less risky than straight-on moves.

Note This Danger

In the same way that we are more likely to be aggressive when we carry a weapon, we are more likely to get physical—and get injured or killed—when we have engaged in physical training. By continually emphasizing Cornerstones 1, 2, and 3 before 4, we will condition ourselves to automatically use mind before body.

From Training to Life

In summary, this chapter teaches how to transform—and emerge unscathed from—a face-off with an armed assailant. The ability to do so is based on these two awarenesses:

- We are given our powerful minds for one reason: to use them.

- Violent confrontation is neither Nature's way nor our inherent Human way to settle differences.

This chapter serves another purpose: Its underlying themes of core skill development and energy alignment echo throughout the book and portray the heart and soul of Guardian Training. These themes are applicable to the whole of life. By fully developing our given talents and using them in alignment with the Greater Good, we show the highest level of honor and respect for our people and our Mother. This, the essence of the Guardian Way, is what I want to leave you with as we conclude this phase of our Training together.

At the same time, this is no "goodbye," as there is no such thing in the Guardian Way. When the members of my Wolfpack rambled off to spend some time alone after a hunt or training exercise, the Wolves and I felt that we were parting only physically. The same was true of the Ojibwe Guardians with whom I trained. When we split up after a Mission, we said, "*Geegawabamin*," which means *We are together until we see each other again.*

To honor this enduring kinship we Guardians have that runs deeper than time and space, I would rather leave you with the following story than say "goodbye." It is an ancient Zen teaching that alone evokes every splendid hue of the spectrum we know as the Guardian Way.

"Halt!"

The woman ignored the growling voice and kept walking down the road.

"Halt, or you will be lying in a pool of your own blood before you take another step!"

Still, the woman kept walking.

The command came from a vicious highwayman who was hidden in the roadside brush. He had robbed and killed many people on the country's isolated stretches of road. Dumbfounded, he watched the woman who, alone and vulnerable, maintained her demeanor and kept on her way.

"Why did you not halt?" he hissed into the woman's face when he caught up to her, grabbed her by the shoulders, and spun her around. "I could have sliced you in half with one lash of my sword!"

"I am like you; I wish to go on living," she replied. "Yet if you want to kill me, I accept that as well. If there is anything you need, I would consider it an honor to help you as I can." The woman then bowed and turned to continue her journey.

The outlaw stood there for a moment, then dropped his sword and followed the woman, who was a wandering beggar. For the next four years, he listened to her every word and observed her every action. Anyone who knows him now would argue vehemently against his supposed past as a bandit whose very existence once instilled bone-chilling fear in every person to travel a lonely road. He now serves the people through his every thought and action—he is their Guardian.

Chapter 27 Citations

1   Charles C. Branas et al., "Investigating the Link Between Gun Possession and Gun Assault," *American Journal of Public Health* 99, no. 11 (November 2009): 2034-40.

2   David Hemenway, Mary Vriniotis, and Matthew Miller, "Is An Armed Society A Polite Society? Guns and Road Rage," *Accident Analysis and Prevention* 38, no. 4 (July 2006): 687-95.

GLOSSARY

alignment consciousness: Awareness of and alignment with the energies present.

Balance: The state of **natural** order and harmonious functioning of an organism or a system.

Be as a question: To live with an openness to all possibilities; to avoid assumptions.

Beauty Way: A way of life that allows one to remain centered and not only see, but also benefit from all in life that appears beyond control.

Becoming: The ability to assume another identity for the purpose of gaining first-hand, intimate knowledge of the feelings, thoughts, motivations, and circumstance of the entity; a progressed form of **Shadowing**.

Buffer Zone: The margin of safety needed to accommodate the unexpected and to allow for error.

Circle: A community that works interdependently rather than hierarchically, recognizing the value and equal importance of every person's role in the group.

Circle consciousness: Heart-generated thinking and feeling that takes into account the **Circle of Life**; allows transcendence of the **ego** to accommodate the needs of others along with personal needs

Circle of Life: The community of Plant, Animal, Mineral and Sky beings who live together in **Balance**.

Circle Way: The manner in which all things are related to, and affect, each other.

Circle Way of thinking: See **integrative thinking**.

Civilized: The lifestyle that results from living out of Balance; characterized by isolation from Nature, environmental degradation, regimentation, hierarchical structures, materialism, and loss of individuality.

confirmation bias: The tendency to search for, interpret, favor, and recall information in a way that affirms one's prior beliefs or hypotheses.

divided thinking: Creating distinct appraisals and value judgments rather than seeing all as interconnected and important in their own right; creates dichotomies and a projected sense of separation in the external world.

Dolfinning: Moving silently and inconspicuously through the water like a Dolphin or Otter rather than paddling over the surface like a Duck.

ego: The aspect of personality that creates self-consciousness and individual identity; our fear-based identity; **ego** dominance can inhibit development of **Guardian Consciousness**.

ego perspective: Seeing the world solely through one's own preferences, beliefs, and limitations, and projecting those onto the external world.

ego-response pattern: The knee-jerk reaction to being inconvenienced; often includes **ego perspective**, argument, conflict, blame, and projection.

Elder: An aged community or clan member who is highly regarded as a bearer of inter-generational clan knowledge; a keeper of traditions; a source of guidance based on wisdom drawn from life experience and ancestral memories.

envision: To mentally create a scenario for the purpose of discovering its characteristics or outcome without needing to directly observe or experience it.

External Communication: Information-sharing with anyone potentially exposed to the **Mission** but not directly related to it.

Greater Good: The best possible outcome for the greatest number of people, regardless of relationship.

Guardian: One who acts as lookout, guard, information gatherer, spy, message bearer, protector, and **Scout**; relays important observations back to the rest of the **pack**; holds to the periphery.

Guardian Consciousness: A limbic-brained way of being in which one steps beyond the **ego** and becomes capable of functioning with others like an organ within an organism; characteristics include a sense of purpose, collaboration, selflessness, alertness, safety, discomfort, open-mindedness, and sharing.

Guardian Diet: Humans' ancestral diet and the optimal approach to nutrition, comprised of foods that are high in fat, high in fiber, moderate in protein, and low in carbohydrates.

Guardian Warrior: The sentry, wayfinder, messenger, ambassador, sleuth, defender, provider, and sibling of the **Circle**; to **Native** People, he or she is the manifestation of courage, selflessness, and desire to serve.

Guardian Way: A mode of being in the world that often involves serving wherever and whenever needed, helping others reach their full potentials, cultivating situational awareness, transcending limiting beliefs, creating options where there are none, and leading lives of bliss.

hard sensory perception: Focused attention, which can help in the immediacy of the moment but cripple situational awareness; a fear-based fight-or-flight survival response; the opposite of **soft sensory perception**.

Heart-of-Hearts: The center of one's being and seat of personal **Balance** where feelings, intuition, ancestral memories, the senses, and mental input come together to give perspective and guidance.

integrative thinking: A process of thinking that can manage tasks while still perceiving the unity, interconnectedness, and equal importance of all things in the external world.

Internal Communication: Information sharing within the **pack**.

Mental Mastery: An approach to life that involves refusing to argue or acknowledge conflict, living with mentally skilled people, and offering to mediate others' apparent conflicts.

Mind-Muscle Memory: Operating on automatic pilot, reverting to the mechanics and awarenesses of **Guardian Training** rather than to judgment based on one's senses, rationale, and conscience.

Mission: An assignment that is treated like a problem to be solved.

Mission Consciousness: The state of mind where one feels an overriding sense of synergy with the group, like an organ within an organism.

Native: A plant or animal living a **natural** life in their **natural** habitat; a person living a hunter-gatherer lifestyle.

Native Lifeway: The lifestyle and teachings of indigenous **Native** Peoples.

natural: Intrinsic to a species or system.

Naturespeak: The mother tongue of all life and the foundation of inter-species communication; the operating system of the mind and the basic lens through which the world is perceived; the root from which spoken and written languages grew.

numb-numb syndrome: Maladaptive neural synapses (the first *numb*) that provoke knee-jerk responses (the second *numb*).

Nurturer: One who tends to the welfare of the pups, acting as babysit-ter, playmate, healthcare provider, and protector; cares for any sick or injured packmates; Human **Nurturers** play parallel roles.

Old Days: The era before **Civilized** culture, when the **Native Lifeway** was common.

Old Way: The lifestyle and practices intrinsic to hunter-gatherers.

pack: A social unit of one voice, one spirit, and one purpose.

Path: The direction of one's life.

peer influence: Impact from peers that supports personal empower-ment and the **Circle Way**; guides the formation of a **pack**; produces the opposite effect of peer pressure.

performance anxiety: The feelings of fear that arise before a **Mission** or other important task.

personal consciousness: A self-centered, rationality-based way of being that can involve expectation, belief, bias, and seeing experi-ences through prior mental filters; contrary to **Mission Conscious-ness**; see **ego**.

Presence Training: An exercise that cultivates awareness, attunement, and adaptability; involves refraining from doing the same thing in the same way more than twice in a row; engaging consciously in whatever the moment presents.

Prevention Training: A way of being designed to prevent automatic responses to life's activities; see **Beauty Way**.

Ruse Training: The practice of using **shadow skills** to create a façade that is believable enough to allow the serving of the **Greater Good** without being detected.

Scout: A person who is sent ahead of the group to gather intelligence for the Mission; see **Guardian**.

Seeker: A person who is attempting to find or obtain something; see **Guardian**.

self-consciousness: See **personal consciousness** and **ego**.

Selfless, Alert, and Safe (SAS): The three states of being each **pack** member must achieve in order to participate in a **Mission**.

Shadow Camp: A ruse that looks like an actual camp, designed to attract enemies and divert them from the **Stealth Camp**.

shadow skills: The ability to create façades, such as **smokescreens**, diversions, false identities, and other deceptions, to help serve the **Greater Good**.

Shadowing: The ability to move under cover and see without being seen; intrinsic to the **Guardian Way**; employed on nearly all **Missions**.

signaling: Transmitting information by means of a gesture, action, or sound.

smokescreen: Façade used to either mask or distract attention from a **Mission**.

soft sensory perception: Dispassionate, broad awareness that does not focus on any particular sight or sound; the opposite of **hard sensory perception**.

song of the track: A chorus of voices that carry on a conversation about who passed by, and when and why.

Stealth Camp: An inconspicuous, temporary settlement that **Guardians** use to complete their **Missions**.

Stealth Consciousness/stealth perspective: A way of being that automatically considers outside risk factors by looking through the eyes of a potential discoverer, with the intention of not being caught.

Switch Training: An exercise that involves having intentions without others discovering said intentions.

thinking-without-thought mind: The limbic process, which is the sensory-feeling center of the brain that does not rate or compare.

training: A way of being in which one develops skills, with no ultimate end point.

Trauma Memory Responses (TMRs): Residual reactions experienced after the traumatic event is over.

Truthspeaking: Concise, straight-from-the-heart expression of personal reality; engenders trust and strengthens relationship.

Voice: The pack's galvanizer and point person; synthesizes information, then directs the **pack's** course of action; speaks and negotiates for the **pack**; in the center of most activities.

Native Terms:

Geegawabamin: (Ojibwe) We are together until we see each other again.

Gichitwa: (Ojibwe) Someone who puts the cares and concerns of others before him or herself.

Gigawabaman: (Ojibwe) You will continue to be seen by me.

Halau: (Polynesian) A *Hula* training school.

Hula: (Polynesian) The chant-dance that served as **Guardian** movement training and the telling of **Guardian** stories.

Kaitiakitanga: (Maori) 'Kai' means food for soul, body, and mind; 'tiaki' refers to caretaking; and 'tanga' is the people, which includes the plant people, the rock people, and the animal people. Describes the role of the **Guardian**.

Kizhenaabeg: (Ojibwe) The benevolent Humans.

Kumu: (Polynesian) An Elder **Guardian** who served as a *Halau* Trainer.

Manaajiidiwin: (Ojibwe) To be respectful and go easy on each other.

Ogichida: (Ojibwe) **Guardian Warrior**.

INDEX

M

Magic Carpet Exercise 150-51
Manaajiidiwin 40, 262
Maori xi, 262
  martial arts 65, 135, 245
  meditation 57, 163-64
  mental health 16
  Mental Mastery 9, 248, 250, 252-53, 259
Mind-Muscle Memory 109-10, 259
mindfulness 21
  mischief 123, 125, 159
  Mission
  approach 58-59, 69, 122, 160, 164, 172
  choice during 84-85
  communication 198
  components 47
  conflict 3, 56, 64-65, 167, 174
  covertness 219-28
  debriefing 180
  defined 46, 179, 259
  disengage from 70
  execution 183, 185-95, 211-18
  failure 123, 125-26, 202
  Mission Consciousness 58, 192-95, 230, 260 (See also under pack)
  mistakes 83
  performance 19, 109-10, 143, 147, 173
  planning 74, 156-57, 164, 203-10
  presence 155
  priorities 48-49, 154, 176
  success 150-51, 165, 250
  signaling (See signaling)
  stealth 169
  take no chances 171
  unlabeled 20
  when discovered 229-34
  Mission Consciousness. See under Mission

N

Native Lifeway ix, 1, 9, 260

natural
  abilities 58, 61
  defined 260
  disaster 3
  cravings 118 (See also diet)
  execution 59
  flow 67
  forces 68
  inclinations 32, 35, 60, 104, 129, 208, 223
  realm 84, 132
  resources 43
  selection 84, 111
  talking 223
natural selection 84, 111
Naturespeak 260
  No-Thumb 67-69
  non-verbal communication 25
numb-numb syndrome 95, 260
Nurturer 23-26, 28-30, 31-32, 34-35, 108, 260
  nuts 115, 117-18, 158

O

Ogichida 38-40, 262, 271
Ojibwe 22, 38-39, 254, 262, 271
  Old Days 24, 260
Old Way 6, 260
organic 116, 210
orienteering 156

P

pack
  alpha pair 26
  archetypal roles in 23, 25, 31
  Coming Together Rituals 210
  conflict between 26-28
  defined 260
  evolution of 139
  functionality of 175, 187-88, 205-206
  how to create 96
  howl 209
  ideal communication 240-41
  living with a pack of wolves 75,

ACKNOWLEDGMENTS

When I went to my Native Elders for guidance or instruction, they would typically tell me, "Go and ask the animals." The Elders said it is where they were sent to learn, and it is where I would best learn, also. I took my yearnings to a pack of Wolves, where Simbut Meaxtkao (Mohican for *Silver Wolf*), Deshum Nashak (Mohican for *Earth Thunderer*) and their kin adopted and trained me. My first expression of gratitude must go to them, as a good share of this book is a literal recounting of what they taught me as we ran together in the pure bliss of the Beauty Way.

Along with my Wolf kin, I want to honor Lac du Flambeau Ojibwe Elder and tribal president Tom Maulson, cultural emissary Nick Hockings, and the other Guardians who trained me to serve with them in the harrowing struggle to restore their treaty rights during the 1987-1991 Walleye War.

Credit for the organization and easy flow of this text goes to Rebecca Lill, who has a unique talent for making something useful out of my ramblings. With his innate Guardian sensitivity, Danny Fletcher helped me choose the material most appropriate for this book. Brett Schwartz, a valued veteran of several of my previous book projects, collaborated with multi-talented Alexandra Steussy-Williams, the Managing Editor of Snow Wolf Publishing, on the glossary, index, and citations. In addition, Alexandra did the final edit. Master transcriber Nan Casper danced most of the text out of my voice recordings, and Elisabeth Demeter (a.k.a. Wild Rose) plied her poetic sense in translating the German edition of this book.

The dedicated Trainees I have been privileged to guide deserve special credit for this book, for without their testing and mirroring, this book would be no more than the fanciful musings of a daydreaming aspirant.

And now I wish to recognize those who made everything possible—my Guardian ancestors, whose talents and tenacities I have inherited. As they live on in me, it is my fondest wish that our work in renewing the Guardian Way find continual and growing expression in the generations to follow.

ABOUT THE AUTHOR

Tamarack Song has been in Guardian Training since he was a young child. His first Missions were rescuing wild animals in distress and protecting kids who were being bullied. He saw himself as Robin Hood righting wrongs as he sleuthed through the neighborhood woods, or Superman serving justice while flying through town on his red Schwinn bike.

Mentored by Wolves when he was a young adult, Tamarack would train with the pups and shadow the pack's Guardians on scouting excursions, boundary patrols, and hunts. In the 1980s, he joined with the Ojibwe Indian Ogichida (Warriors) during the Wisconsin Walleye War, which was waged to reassert the Ojibwe's treaty-guaranteed rights to hunt and gather on their ceded territories. In honor of his service, Tamarack was given the title "Ogichida Tamarack" by the Lac du Flambeau Ojibwe Wa-Swa-Gon Treaty Association.

Now in his seventies, Tamarack still maintains an active personal training schedule; and he runs at-home and on-the-ground training intensives for those called to the Guardian Way.

Printed in Great Britain
by Amazon

62907232R00170